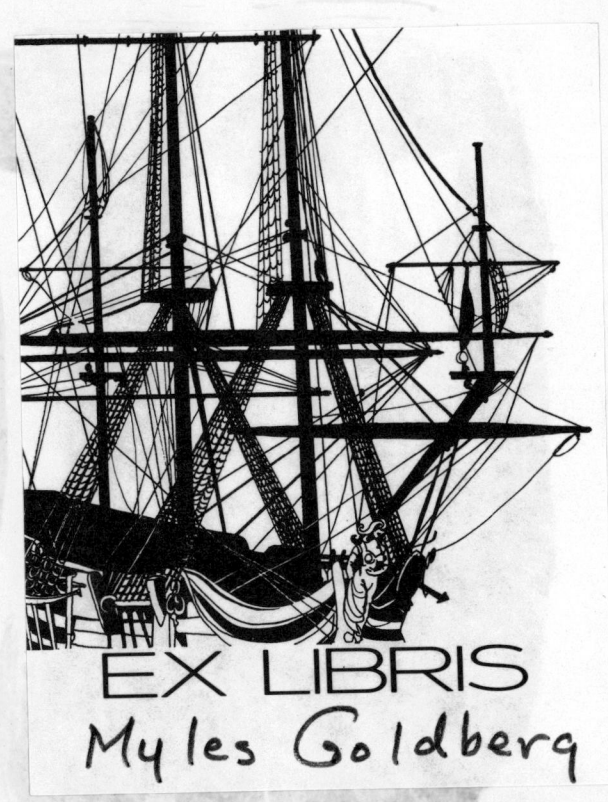

MANAGEMENT by TASK FORCES

A Manual on the Operation of Interdisciplinary Teams

Lawrence W. Bass
Consultant, formerly Vice President
Arthur D. Little, Inc.
Washington, D. C.

Lomond Books
Mt. Airy, Maryland
1975

Copyright © 1975 by Lomond Systems, Inc. No part of this book may be reproduced in hardcopy, electronic or other form unless permission is secured from the copyright holder.

The quotations in Chapter Two from Peter F. Drucker, "The Practice of Management" (Harper and Row, New York, Copyright 1954) and in Chapter Six from Harold Koontz and Cyril O'Donnell, "Principles of Management" (Fourth Edition, McGraw-Hill Book Company, New York, Copyright 1968) are used with the permission of the respective publishers and authors

LC Catalog Number 74-82702

ISBN:
   Clothbound 0-912338-09-1
   Microfiche   0-912338-10-5

Lomond Systems, Inc.
Mt. Airy, Maryland 21771

SUMMARY

Technical leadership among organizations or nations is not solely tied to the size of the research and development effort. It is greatly helped by the orderly use of a mix of skills to carry an idea forward from conception to practical utility. Task forces based on interdisciplinary principles are an excellent management tool for moving projects toward completion surely and speedily. The techniques of task force management are broadly applicable to all activities aimed at innovation, from the development of a new product to staging a play.

This monograph has the aim of explaining in detail the organization and operation of such task forces. It gives information on the value of this modern technique to industrial firms, public agencies, and developing countries. It contains many specific examples of the composition, program, and managerial control of teams in these domains. All procedures described have been put to the test of practical use by my associates and myself in our consulting work and in many cases have been adopted at least in principle by a number of our clients. The book as a whole lends itself to training courses in interdisciplinology, and earlier versions of the material have been so used.

Composite task forces are a relatively recent managerial device for solving problems by coordinated exercise of a diversity of skills under the guidance of a team leader. This technique counterbalances the inertia of cellular organizations which are being spawned by increasing specialization of expertise.

Task forces are often used in industry and government to meet situations of crisis, but when the emergency has passed the lessons of success are forgotten. Management reverts to its former structured dispersal of resources of specialized manpower into isolated units and is obliged to effect co-ordination through successive layers of supervision.

In industry, interdisciplinary teams are being increasingly used for new product development. The most effective form of task force for this purpose is a group of specialists under a leader who is responsible for coordinating the use of their skills. Because of changes in the pattern of required expertise at successive major stages on the road to commercialization, a short sequence of interlocking teams is employed to carry the concept forward through product and process definition; market estimation; product, process, market, and cost-benefit confirmation; to final approval by top management for commercialization. Criteria of feasibility are applied with increasing stringency, as information accumulates, to avoid wastage of effort on projects that turn out to be unpromising. The makeup of these successive teams stimulates both feed-back of information to take care of needed changes, and feed-forward to prepare later participants for their roles in the total effort.

Task forces are being adopted to plan corporate development and diversification by systematic comparison of the merits of alternative opportunities. They are valuable, for example, for feasibility studies, sales and production planning, plant location projects, and the improvement of technical programs. By budgeting the use of skills, and hence costs, they optimize the deployment of a company's most valuable resource, namely, its trained manpower.

A favorable climate must be created within an organization to reap the full benefits of interdisciplinology. The structure must be loose and fluent to encourage whole-hearted individual participation in team activities. The delegation of responsibility and authority to the task force must be much more liberal, subject only to general supervision but not to actual direction. This freedom of action is in strong contrast to the traditional managerial hierarchy. It requires the channels of the informal organization, while the formal structure assumes the housekeeping function of placing the individual in proper relation to his colleagues. The appendix gives practical procedures for introducing task force methodology.

Projects in the public sector, too, benefit from the use of interdisciplinary principles. The teams are usually made up of government employees, but their effectiveness can be increased by outside advisors from technology and the managerial and financial communities. There is need for much improvement in techniques to take into consideration the views of the general public, the presumed beneficiaries of the undertakings.

National planning agencies in developing countries can greatly improve their effectiveness by using interdisciplinary teams to increase the incisiveness of selection of industrial sectors which are promising areas for expansion, and in formulating government activities to stimulate this growth. Here, too, mechanisms are important to secure advice from the private sector on technologic, entrepreneurial, and financial matters.

Task forces stimulate group entrepreneurship which inspires the staff members to full use of their talents and creativity. The organization as a whole becomes a dynamic body which boldly faces the challenge of the future.

CONTENTS

Summary _____ iii

List of Tables _____ xi

List of Charts _____ xii

Preface _____ xiii

Chapters

One Task Force Concepts _____ 1

Task forces to meet emergencies—The evolution of interdisciplinary management—Distinction between task forces and committees—Information transfer in task force systems

Two Categories of Interdisciplinary Activities ___ 11

Relationships among the participating group—Comparison of the five categories—Unoriented unstructured discussions—Oriented unstructured collaborations—Oriented structured programs without constraints—Oriented structured projects with constraints—Projects under executive direction—Introduction of interdisciplinary techniques into large meetings

Three Task Forces for New Product Development ___ 23

Criteria of feasibility for new products under development—Prerequisites for task force operation—Selection of team leaders—Planning the interdisciplinary team—Organization of the team—Team activities—Report on completion of the project—Con-

	tinuing activity in later stages—Co-ordination of long-range research with applied projects	
Four	Task Forces for Successive Stages	39
	Co-ordination of successive project teams—Progressive application of criteria of feasibility—Types of responsibilities in successive task forces—System of stages and steps in product development—Short-cuts in the use of the list of development steps	
Five	Managerial Control of Task Force Systems	61
	Time accounting for major projects—Budgetary control of projects—Control of minor assignments by consolidation—Management of non-project activities—Systematic deployment of staff efforts	
Six	Environment and Benefits of Interdisciplinary Teams	73
	Contrasting patterns of responsibility and authority—Interdisciplinary teams and management theory——Benefits of interdisciplinary systems	
Seven	Task Forces for Corporate Development	85
	A systematic program for corporate development—Assessment of internal resources—Formulation of plans for growth——Appraisal of growth opportunities	
Eight	Task Forces for Other Corporate Functions	101
	Engineering activities—Plant location studies—Sales and production scheduling—Feasibility studies—Market development	

	—Pollution abatement—Technical audits—Laboratory location—Quality control—Handling of complaints—Trouble-shooting—Accounting summaries—Reporting systems—Process engineering—Market research on new products—Job enrichment in repetitive tasks—The distribution of executive efforts	
Nine	Projects in the Public Domain	117
	Methodology—Sources of diversified expertise—Essentials in relationships with consultants—Examples of public projects—Public technology—Techniques to obtain a consensus of public opinion	
Ten	The Environment for Industrial Expansion	131
	Provision of a government focus for industrial development—Government measures to stimulate industrial development—Statistical information—Framing industrial development policies and programs—Policies for technology——Government measures to strengthen development resources	
Eleven	A Systems Approach to Economic Development	141
	Methodology—Preliminary trial of the procedures on accumulated ideas—Compilation of an array of industrial micro-sectors—Selection and definition of evaluation criteria—Screening procedures for selecting favorable micro-sectors—Critical appraisal of selected micro-sectors—Decision on courses of action—Estimation of total impact of new industrial ventures—Combination of	

	industrial growth with other major economic elements—General comments on the procedures—Methodology in an industrial development study in Lebanon	
Twelve	Implementation of Development Opportunities	161
	Government activities to assist implementation—Responsibilities of entrepreneurs—Requirements for government promotion and entrepreneurial action—Summary	
Appendix	How to Start Task Force Systems	173
	Typical questions about the feasibility of task forces—Prerequisites for task force systems—Practical demonstration of task force methodology—The aftermath	
	Collateral Reading	183
	Index	193
	Biography of the Author	197

List of Tables

1. Interdisciplinary functions in a product development team ... 6
2. Advantages and disadvantages of different categories of interdisciplinary activities ... 15
3. Form of project outline ... 28
4. Composition of a task force to develop a novel cereal product ... 30
5. Distribution of skills in a task force ... 32
6. Work record of an individual ... 64
7. Estimate of time distribution for a disciplinary group ... 71
8. Comparative benefits and risks of new items, innovative new products, and new product lines ... 91
9. Screening of new product opportunities ... 95
10. Screening Procedure for Development Opportunities ... 149
11. Estimated impact of new ventures on the industrial economy ... 153
12. Incorporation of projected industrial growth into the national master plan ... 155

List of Charts

I. Information transfer in a cellular organization as compared with a task force _____ 9

II. Progressive application of technoeconomic criteria _____ 41

III. Representation of disciplines in successive task forces _____ 45

IV. Organizational structure for task forces _____ 75

V. Requirements for government promotion and entrepreneurial action _____ 167

PREFACE

When I entered industrial work as a technical director over 40 years ago, I was struck by the need for closer cooperation with operating departments of the company. My associates and I arranged to have representatives of manufacturing and sales participate in project reviews and in the formulation of our entire program. We used an elementary form of interdisciplinary teams to carry out all our activities, including introduction of new processes on a commercial scale. I followed these principles in other industrial positions which I held subsequently.

About 20 years later, when I joined Arthur D. Little, I found there a task force system which went beyond any I have seen elsewhere. All work done for clients is carried out by interdisciplinary teams; today, with a technical staff of about 800, work on several hundred client assignments is going forward continuously. Experience has made the formation and control of project teams such a matter of habit that the procedures are carried out with a minimum of strain on the individual or the organization. Monitoring of "overhead activities"—a vital precaution to secure optimum allocation of technical skills—is carried out by a scheme similar to that described in this book.

This monograph is my personal interpretation of how this experience may be most useful to industry and to public agencies. Consultation with a wide variety of clients on the management of research and development and on corporate planning and development has given me a chance to work with quite a number of them in adopting or improving task force systems. This background in the problems they encounter has been valuable in trying to find general solutions. It has also convinced me that these same principles can be applied with benefit much more widely.

In recent years my attention has been turned to the difficult questions involved in economic betterment of developing countries. I have taken part in the activities of a number of them, chiefly under the aegis of The Ford Foundation, Inter-American Development Bank, National Academy of Sciences, United Nations Industrial Development Organization, and U.S. AID. Task forces are a systematic way to attack many of their problems to obtain optimum mixes of skills for planning, feasibility studies, and transfer of technology. Thorough evaluation of proposed projects to insure practicality is urgently needed to conserve scarce resources of trained manpower and financial support. Gratifyingly enough, some organizations, particularly some technologic institutes in developing countries, have begun to adopt interdisciplinary approaches.

In writing this book I have the advantage of having written a number of articles on different aspects of task force methodology. On these I have drawn freely.

I owe much to many friends, especially my associates at Arthur D. Little, for ideas gleaned during discussions of the principles and practice of interdisciplinology.

Washington
May 1974   L.W.B.

CHAPTER ONE
TASK FORCE CONCEPTS *

Task Forces to Meet Emergencies. Business firms and government agencies resort often to task forces to respond to crises. In industry, the emergency may be due to the loss of production capacity, to the threat of competitive innovation, or to drastic change in the economic climate. In public affairs, new problems affecting the community may urgently require solution. In all these cases, answers of adequate scope obviously call for consolidated efforts and conclusions of a composite team of specialists.

In an industrial emergency, the chief executive calls together senior representatives of the major departments to organize a crash attack. The problem is analyzed, possible remedies are weighed, and a plan of action is adopted. Highest priority is given to the program. The diverse skills of the organization are mobilized, coordination of all activities is exerted by top management, and in due course the selected response to the threat is put into operation.

This is a typical example of the merits of a coordinated attack on a major problem, to draw upon the collective talents and resources of the firm. The stress of the emergency calls forth vigorous efforts from all sides, under the eye of the top management. Initiative and creative thinking are encouraged. Channels of communication are forced open among operating departments and staff groups. The organization is operating as a whole instead of as a collection of isolated units. Necessity breaks down the barriers between cells of responsibility and expertise.

But when the crisis has passed, the object lesson is all too often for-

---

* Interdisciplinary activities are classified in five categories in Chapter Two, according to the degree of orientation and structuring. Task forces are those in which the efforts of the group are coordinated toward the solving of a defined task. Emphasis throughout this book is on the type (IV) defined as "oriented structured projects with constraints." This is the most effective for attacking a practical objective because the entire program is coordinated by a team leader who is responsible for the amount of effort from each member and for maintenance of the project schedule.

In the text the terms "Task Force" and "Interdisciplinary Team" are, therefore, used interchangeably to denote this general kind of orderly use of diverse skills.

gotten. "Management-as-usual" follows its disjointed course. The bureaucracy of separate functions falls again into its routine style. Communications resume their formal patterns. Initiative is damped by layers of supervision further and further removed from the site of action. The organization loses its sense of urgency.

The author is convinced that a spirit of common entrepreneurship can be introduced into an organization without the whiplash of an emergency. Procedures have been developed by which the cellular relationships can be converted into a dynamic system of task forces. This provides a stirring climate for individual responsibility and initiative.

The Evolution of Interdisciplinary Management

Military Operations. In my opinion the beginnings of interdisciplinology were thrust by circumstances on the armed forces, which would seem to be an unlikely breeding ground because of their characteristically rigid structure.

In Homeric accounts, warfare was largely a series of combats between pairs of combatants. About the beginning of the seventh century B.C., differentiation of types of weapons and the unwieldy size of armies brought about a degree of organization and timing of battle entry which Herodotus attributes to the Medes. The king-generals began to think about the deployment and scheduling of light and heavy infantry, light and heavy cavalry, archers, slingers, charioteers, elephant and camel cohorts, and later of contraptions for hurling missiles. Because of their autocratic rule, their decision making was anything but the relaxed interchanges of views we hope for in modern task forces.

The Greek forces, on the other hand, were usually made up of many independent units with similar weapons. Strategy and tactics were selected on the basis of open debate among the captains, and in the case of the march of the Ten Thousand, for example, the debate was carried out in meetings of the entire forces.

The Romans brought additional system to the organization and use of different military skills. But very often the leader was setting an example of personal prowess in the forefront of combat. It took many centuries for generals to realize that the best place to use their brains was at some distant observation point. And even then their commanders were dispersed with their commands instead of being at

Task Force Concepts

hand for counsel. The staff officers were engaged chiefly in carrying orders to the various units.

A high point in military interdisciplinology was the concept for the general staff in modern times. These officers had no responsibilities for field command. Instead they planned the details, large and small, of entire campaigns.

In World War II technical task forces became recognized as an essential resource for military innovation in a host of applications. Prime examples are: operations research to determine optimum convoy organization and flight patterns for anti-submarine searches; development of science-based hardware, including network analysis to coordinate the diverse inputs; and the consummate blending of skills which led to atomic weapons. With this proof of value, interdisciplinary techniques have become an indispensable part of resources for defense.

Civilian Affairs. There are some glimmerings of organized production operations in ancient times. The true factory system, however, is a phenomenon of the last few centuries.

In the erection of such great structures as the cathedrals, the master builder was in full command. He must have allowed some latitude to his staff of artists in stone, because the detail was too great for a single man to handle.

The early factories of the industrial revolution were enlargements of family controlled businesses for making a limited line of products. The owner-managers were in full control, and in keeping with the philosophy of the day probably did not often seek the opinions of their employees.

Engineering Projects. The first use of task forces in the modern sense began about one hundred years ago in large construction projects. As civilian engineering assignments became progressively more complex, engineers started to develop managerial techniques for systematic coordination of the inputs of a group of diversified specialists. The chief project engineer recruited a team of individual experts, planned with them a collaborative program to make use of the spectrum of their skills, provided general overseeing for their individual activities, and then consolidated all the work into a finished job.

The management of this collection of talents was helped by two factors. First, the participants used a common technical jargon and had a common practical point of view. Second, they had all been trained to use a systematic attack consisting of analyzing requirements, planning a program, estimating the costs of the facility they were designing, and then living within these estimates.

These managerial skills have been adopted and perfected in large independent firms of engineering contractors and in the internal engineering departments of other organizations. The administrative advantages of this task force approach were accepted in a matter-of-fact manner because it was the engineering way of doing things. These techniques have, however, attracted too little attention as broad principles to be applied more widely as a mechanism for problem solving.

Industrial Consultants. Groups of consultants found several decades ago that interdisciplinary management was a very important aid in carrying out various types of assignments. Many of them were engineers, who had seen the advantages of this system for conducting construction projects. When adapted to handling a wider range of problems, it enabled them to give more comprehensive techno-economic services to their clients. Also, they developed the internal control procedures for allocation of skills.

The rapid growth of management consultancy has resulted in the extension of the scientific method to a wide range of general business problems. Many of the practitioners were trained as engineers or technologists but have concentrated their talents on the management sciences rather than their original disciplines. In later examples it will be pointed out that many task force assignments have important technologic aspects as well as those on the managerial side. In my opinion, the solutions will be improved by inclusion of practicing engineers or technologists as well as management specialists.

Research and Development. In earlier days, concepts for new products and processes were often carried through from research and development phases to commercialization by the entrepreneurial drive of an individual versatile technologist. Without using a formal task force, he called on the skills of his associates to help him test his prototype process on large-scale equipment, prepare samples for interested customers, and eventually start a new business, of which he frequently became the head. As technical departments became larger, the structures became more elaborate because of increase of specialization in the staff. How could entrepreneurship be restored? Consulting firms, for example, are often asked by clients not only to develop a new product but also to provide justification on the basis of manufacturing feasibility and market potential. The task force procedures developed by engineering contractors provide a good model for carrying out such assignments. In more recent years, internal research departments in many private and public organizations have been adopting this scheme of management.

Resarch and development projects present very good examples of the procedures for organizing, operating, and controlling diversified task forces. First, they should be made up of a wider range of disciplinary specialists than is currently used for other types of problems. Second, as the first stage in a succession of major steps on the path from concept to commercialization, they should provide for effective liaison with other corporate functions. Research and development projects will therefore be used freely for illustration in later chapters, with the assumption that the same principles and methodology are applicable to other activities.

At this point it seems appropriate to introduce the structure of a team of this kind as an example. Table 1 shows the make-up and functions of the members for the initial technologic stage of product development. The upper part of the tabulation lists in the first column the four key members, then their responsibilities, and finally the relative amounts of effort planned for them. Because the brunt of the work lies in applied research, the team leader is usually an experienced technologist from that section. The scope of interaction with still other departments during the progress of the work, to help guide the program toward practical utility, is shown in the bottom part of the table.

Feasibility Studies. Before making commitments for the expense of large projects, private firms and public agencies find it a wise precaution to have comprehensive technoeconomic feasibiilty studies carried out. These require a combination of skills for what is basically an engineering approach. Often they are entrusted to consultants, particularly to obtain objective judgment free from internal biases or enthusiasms. Task force principles provide the proper framework for effective evaluation.

Table 1
INTERDISCIPLINARY FUNCTIONS IN A PRODUCT DEVELOPMENT TEAM
(Technologic Stage)

Key Team	Function	Extent of Participation
Team Leader Technologist	Project definition, program plan, selection and indoctrination of other members, coordination of all work, additional liaison preparatory for further development and implementation	Major effort
Evaluation Specialist	Selection and application of test methodology, establishment of tentative specifications.	Substantial effort
Process Specialist	Advice on process feasibility, preliminary process flow diagrams, initial estimate of facilities requirements and production costs	Participation as needed
Marketing Specialist	Advice on market size and structure, competitive situation, pricing, marketing channels, and costs	Participation as needed
Other Desirable Coordination		
Management	Conformance of concept with corporate plans	Written policy or tentative approval
Other Technical Specialists	Additional specialized information as required	Consultation
Production and Engineering	Feasibility of process, facilities, economics	Preliminary opinion
Marketing	Character of marketing program	Preliminary opinion
Purchasing	Availability and cost of raw materials	Preliminary information
Legal	Pertinent regulations and patents	Preliminary survey

Task Force Concepts

Corporate Development. Many enlightened companies have established corporate planning and development departments to serve in a staff capacity to top management. These groups are found useful to assist in the formulation of policies and plans for growth and for evaluating individual projects in comparison with alternative opportunities. As the value of their services becomes apparent, there is a temptation for them to be expanded in size, but the wise solution is to use them as spearheads for task forces recruited from other departments, rather than to increase their own roster of skills. In this way, they spread the concepts of organized planning, programming, and efficient use of expertise throughout the organization.

Other Opportunities for the Use of Task Forces. Today the term interdisciplinary attack has become a magic phrase because of the obvious need for a combination of talents for solving major socio-techno-economic problems such as environmental pollution and urban decay. Alert managers in organizations with experience in operating task force systems will find many avenues for cooperation in these vitally important activities. It is therefore very timely to study in detail the nature and the potential of this administrative technique.

Distinction Between Task Forces and Committees

Some readers will say that the example of a task force to meet an industrial emergency represents merely a closely knit management committee. This comment may have some validity, but the character of most committees differs widely from the task force activities described in this monograph.

Committees are concerned chiefly with assessment of information made available to them for the purpose of reaching conclusions. The members hold scheduled meetings, but interaction among them at other times is often scanty or absent. They may of course need new information to carry out their responsibilities, and for this purpose they may require some form of task force. They are, in general, deliberative bodies rather than generators of facts.

Task forces, on the other hand, are aggressively oriented. The members develop needed information in their respective spheres. They communicate their findings and conclusions to their colleagues on a timely schedule in order that the others may take them into consideration in carrying out their own missions. Their contacts are frequent and mutually helpful. They participate in discussions to dovetail their common and individual progress toward main objectives. They are an integrated community.

Information Transfer in Task Force Systems

The great benefit of task forces rests on the vast improvement they bring about in information transfer. This includes both the feed-back of new requirements and the feed-forward of accumulated data and interpretations. The superiority in these respects of interdisciplinary teams over cellular organizations is illustrated by Chart I, which shows the interchanges in the development of a new product.

I can anticipate the complaints of critics that the left-hand part of the table is a gross exaggeration of fumbling in a development project. In reply I can only state that I have seen many worse cases, including those in which an investigation was carried to the end by this roundabout route, only to be abandoned because of some overlooked obstacle. If those who initially differ will honestly examine their own experiences, I think most of them will turn up similar instances.

As a specific example I offer the kitchen-testing of food products under development. The test kitchens have historically been located in the advertising department to prepare attractive displays for photographing, to develop household recipes, and to handle inquiries from housewives. As a means of saving expense, the applied research laboratories were not encouraged to install their own kitchens; the researchers had to rely on tests in their own homes, where enthusiasm was likely to lull any suspicions of difficulties in use. As a result, many projects moved far down the channels of development before someone thought it would be a good thing to send samples to the test kitchen, usually located in the main office at a considerable distance from the laboratory. The home economist often found that the product needed reformulation to adapt it to the requirements of the average home, and sometimes the project had to be dropped because it proved to be too difficult to make the necessary changes. As a result of sad experiences of this type, most food technology laboratories now have their own test kitchens staffed by home economists who use the same criteria of domestic convenience as do those in the advertising departments.

CHART I
INFORMATION TRANSFER IN A CELLULAR ORGANIZATION AS COMPARED WITH A TASK FORCE SYSTEM

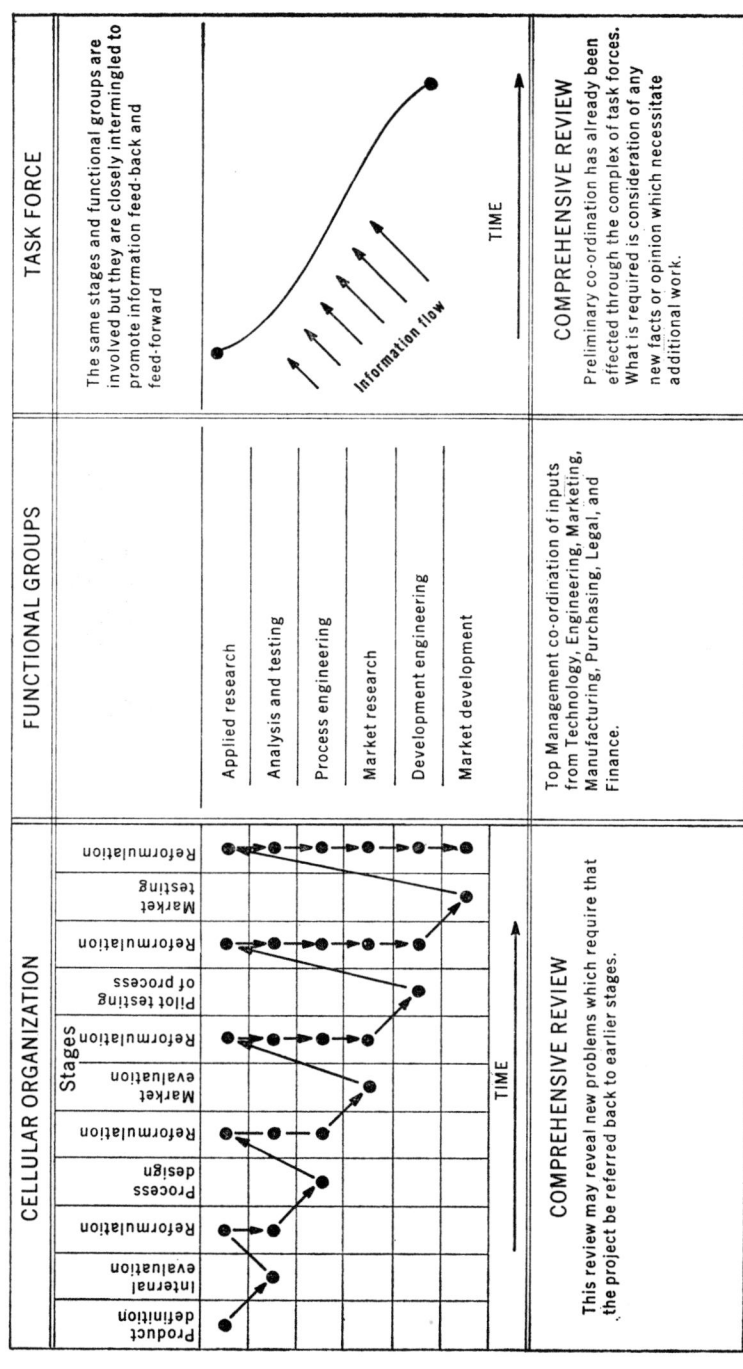

CHAPTER TWO

CATEGORIES OF INTERDISCIPLINARY ACTIVITIES

The intricacy of the problems of a rapidly changing world has aroused widespread interest in interdisciplinary approaches. In space and defense technology, the concrete objectives of designing very complicated hardware have encouraged the development of systems engineering to coordinate the varied inputs of specialized skills. Similarly, the importance of less easily defined goals in the sector of social problems has stimulated corresponding ideas, particularly in public and academic circles.

Many discussions among representatives of different disciplines turn out to be frustrating and unproductive. While there is much lip service to the concept of the necessity for collaboration among specialists, all too often there is little positive interaction. The advocates of each field of knowledge proclaim its importance to the subject but neglect to concern themselves with how it can be meshed constructively with others.

It is apparent that the ground rules for interdisciplinary cooperation are not adequately defined. The situation needs to be corrected so that the expectations for results from such discussions may be realistic. If the participants do not understand the advantages and disadvantages of different modes of interaction, they cannot organize themselves in such a way as to achieve desirable performance.

These experiences point to the need for a general classification of interdisciplinary activities so that the participants have a better comprehension of the strengths and weaknesses of the manner in which they are operating. This should provide a basis for considering the type appropriate for a specific environment and situation. In my opinion, the essential differences lie in the extent of orientation and structuring. This reasoning led me to the description of five categories discussed in detail below:

I. **Unoriented unstructured discussions**: characteristically exhortative, common in seminars regarding the need and opportunities for interaction among disciplines.
II. **Oriented unstructured collaborations**: voluntary associations

of groups of specialists to work independently toward a general objective.

III. **Oriented structured programs without constraints**: activities of volunteers who concur in planned courses of individual efforts to reach a common goal, but without enforceable obligations for performance and schedule.

IV. **Oriented structured projects with constraints**: undertakings in which a project leader is accorded general control over objectives, programs, allocations of effort, and schedules, with acceptance of his authority of leadership by the other participants; the obligations are often, but not necessarily, enforced as a result of responsibility to outside sponsors.

V. **Projects under executive direction**: interdisciplinary activities with direct managerial control of content and performance, frequently employed in the implementation of projects to secure more efficient reduction to practice.

There are, however, no sharp boundaries between these major categories. Each has advantages or disadvantages for a particular case. Indeed, more than one of them may come into play during a single meeting, as the following example illustrates. A joint discussion of surgeons and engineers to consider an integrated approach to a novel prosthetic device (Type II) may require general review of the diversity of skills required (Type I), from which may emerge a consolidated program outline with specified goal (Type III), and this may be converted into a project proposal for outside support (Type IV), including definition of objective, justification of utility, designation of project leader and other team members, structured program, target date, and budget. Finally, to use the results when the investigation has been completed, an entrepreneurial manager may be needed with authority to coordinate implementation (Type V).

Emphasis will be placed throughout this monograph on Type IV, oriented structured projects with constraints, because this is the regime under which task forces can most effectively carry out problem solving. The necessity for relying on the other types to set the stage for organization of these project teams will in general be assumed, although specific needs for them as preliminary steps will be mentioned wherever it seems appropriate.

Interdisciplinary Categories

Relationships Among the Participating Group

Some general comments on the characteristics of interdisciplinary activities will help to explain the differences among the five categories. These relate chiefly to the effect of size, style of leadership, and communication procedures.

The size of the primary group which organizes and oversees the collective effort has a major impact on effectiveness. In practice, a key team of limited membership—from three to not more than six—is likely to be able to reach workable consensus, whereas a larger number often flounders in trying to attain accommodation of an excessive number of individual points of view. The members of this group should be selected to give broad representation of the major component disciplines, both to make the approach to the problem comprehensive, and to satisfy the other participants that the significance of their potential contributions is recognized. The problem of size is particularly serious in Types I and II because of lack of formal structuring, but the same difficulty applies in organizing teams of Types III and IV.

Even without formal structuring, some type of leadership usually arises through tacit acceptance of the influence of dominant figures. The style of operation of these individuals, whether they be appointed or de facto, is a potent factor in the success of the activity. They should take a middle ground between overt dominance and loose permissiveness, in order to inspire the allegiance of the participants and to maintain orderly accomplishment.

The pattern of communication is likewise very significant. Because the ultimate product of team activities is usually written summaries of conclusions, those who are given responsibility for planning and preparing the documentation have an important impact on the effectiveness of interchange of information and opinions.

Comparison of the Five Categories

The relative characteristics of the five types of interdisciplinary activities are summarized in Table 2. The succeeding sections discuss each type in more detail.

The categories are seen from the table to be in descending order of freedom of self-determination of constituent programs, and in increasing order of effectiveness in channeling efforts toward carrying out a defined mission. Their applicabilities to a given objective at a given time should be examined with respect to the environment in which they are to operate and the urgency of positive action.

Types I and II are particularly common in an academic climate and in long range research because they embrace the policy of freedom of individual choice which is inherent in unstructured groups. They stress the importance of personal creativity in uncovering new knowledge.

Type V, on the other hand, occurs frequently in industrial and public organizations which adhere to the classical pattern of a hierarchy in their structures. Characteristically, they assume the form of a pyramid of responsibility and authority. Their weakness when this concept is carried too far is that the need to provide constructive interaction of disciplines forces the management function to higher levels to take care of the required span of control of component skills. Relief of this over-concentration of decision making may be accomplished by various devices for improving liaison by means of coordinating functions.

Type III is a compromise between the looseness of Types I and II versus the direct managerial control of Type V. Its effectiveness is weakened in that the team leader is not given authority to require the members to adhere to agreed programs and schedules. Instead, he has to rely on persuasive measures.

Deficiencies in the rate and directions of progress which may occur in Type III teams can be corrected by the use of Type IV structures. Here the managerial functions of the team leader are reenforced by an external obligation, either to higher management levels or to an outside agency. This is the category which, with optional strictness of control, is tending to be the preferred procedure in industrial and public organizations which are under stress to produce tangible evidence of performance.

Unoriented Unstructured Discussions (Type I)

Many interdisciplinary meetings are being organized in academic circles and in the public sector. These are sometimes limited to very specific topics, but more usually they provide a forum for the expression of individual views on broad problems, such as environmental pollution, urban decay, assistance to developing countries, unrest among students, or the objectives of the educational system, in all of which there are widely divergent opinions regarding methods of

Table 2
ADVANTAGES AND DISADVANTAGES OF DIFFERENT CATEGORIES OF INTERDISCIPLINARY ACTIVITIES

	Advantages	Disadvantages
Type I Unoriented unstructured discussions	Starting point for more specific concepts; develop better understanding and liaison among disciplines; clarify the roles of disciplines in joint undertakings	Rarely lead directly to specific benefits; because of discursiveness consume energy and time
Type II Oriented unstructured collaborations	Encourage collaboration among specialists; stimulate initiative and creativity	Focus of activity not well clarified; contributions and timing uncertain
Type III Oriented structured programs without constraints	Provide channels for diverse inputs with common focus; encourage communications among disciplines	Permit divergence from planned objective and schedule because leadership decisions may not be enforceable
Type IV Oriented structured projects with constraints	Stimulate direct communication and interaction among specialists; result in consensus of competent opinions; performance is regulated by authority of team leader	Program restricted by selection of specialized inputs and managerial style of team leader; adherence to original concept may deter innovation
Type V Projects under executive direction	Lead to direct accomplishment; all inputs under central administrative and operational control	Results depend on ability of executive; initiative and creativity limited by his decisions

solution.

They provide channels for airing the scope of the questions and the areas of expertise which are involved in their confrontation. They promote contacts among specialists in different fields, which often lead to more direct collaboration. They expose the variety of technical jargons to scrutiny, hopefully to stimulate greater mutual understanding.

By themselves, they are unlikely to result directly in concrete programs unless skillful leaders are able to formulate general recommendations which meet with consensus. They may lead to more specific undertakings with a defined orientation and structure. They are therefore a valuable first step in exploring the needs for interdisciplinary activities.

Discussions of this type are frequently organized with unrealistic expectations that definite programs will arise spontaneously from the mere act of establishing a medium of contact among specialists. This is unlikely to occur unless some mechanism is established to enhance collaboration and orientation. For this purpose the use of small working groups in conjunction with the general discussions is advantageous. Their interactions will often lead to the development of concepts which can be undertaken by one of the other categories of interdisciplinary activities.

To summarize, unoriented unstructured discussions are exhortative in nature, inchoate in commitment of participants, and indefinite in leadership.

Oriented Unstructured Collaborations (Type II)

Representatives of different disciplines may join voluntarily to attack a problem which is outlined by mutual agreement among the participants. Informal leadership often centers around what is admitted to be the dominant area of specialization or in the individual who has originated the concept. Commitments to take part are optional and are not formally structured, but are left to each participant to decide on the basis of his interpretation of the needed input from his particular skill. Opinions among the group are openly expressed, but acceptance of the views of others is by persuasion and not by consensus. If it appears that some member is not going to provide the input deemed necessary, another may be added to fill the gap.

Interdisciplinary Categories

The same type of problems mentioned under Type I may be subjects of collaboration, but the objective has now become more specific. For example, a group interested in environmental pollution will decide to concentrate on atmospheric aspects. A physicist and a chemist will volunteer to investigate the most feasible methods for determining the quantity and composition of major pollutants. A climatologist will undertake the study of atmospheric conditions which influence the appearance of undesirable levels. A public health specialist will agree to investigate the physiological effects of major contaminants, and a public administrator will consider possible regulatory measures.

The freedom of this association places emphasis on individual interest and creativity, but the extent and timing of the respective contributions are likely to be casual and unpredictable. The physicist and chemist in this example may become so engrossed in perfecting methodology that identification of the major offending substances is delayed, with the result that suitable data are not available for public health and regulatory studies. On the other hand, under the stimulus of the joint problem there may be developed new techniques for collecting and analyzing the pollutants, although this still leaves a gap in timing.

Better communications and coordination would have given advance notice of the departure from plan, but in this type of interdisciplinary activity agreements of contributors are not binding. In other words, commitments by participants to maintain program and schedule are vague, leadership is opportunistic, and any authority the leader may exert is limited to persuasion or by substitution of other members.

Oriented Structured Programs Without Constraints (Type III)

This category is reached when the members of the group are willing to discipline themselves to accept an organized plan to perform the individual tasks on schedule. They serve under a chairman whom they select to coordinate the group effort. His authority is limited to whatever judgments they are willing to accept and act upon. He can often bring to bear the added influence of the joint opinions of the other participants to insure progress toward the common goal.

Superficially the teams look like Type IV projects. Their operation is much less sure, however, because commitments of the members to program and schedule are voluntary, and the leadership is informal and discretionary in that it lacks the power to enforce performance.

Oriented Structured Projects With Constraints (Type IV)

This is the type of activity which is most effective for reaching a goal when the participants recognize a responsibility to adhere to a program to which they agreed when they joined the team. Their performance is an essential part of the commitment which was made when the program was authorized. If they are unable or unwilling to carry out their parts, they should withdraw so that someone else can fill the gap.

The strongest form of constraint is an obligation to an outside agency. This reenforces the authority of the leader to insist that the necessary inputs should be made in accordance with the agreement or contract with which they are all familiar, because it was basic to their acceptance of team membership. While the leader is the one who bears the public onus, each member must recognize his own share in the responsibility.

This is the form of interdisciplinary attack used by many successful industrial organizations. The constraints arise through the procedures employed to obtain approval for proposed projects, for example, in research and development. These include not only appraisal by research management, but frequently also some type of endorsement in principle from the operating departments which are going to use the results, and from top management which will have to authorize the resources of personnel and financial support for the program.

The managerial techniques are discussed in detail in later chapters. Here, however, it seems appropriate to list the general principles:

1. **Organization:** Responsibility is delegated to a team leader to assemble and coordinate the activities of a group of specialists with the skills required to carry out the assignment authorized by approval of the project outline. Membership usually crosses the lines of the cellular administrative organization and service is frequently on a parttime basis.

2. **Operation:** The team operates as a unit under the leadership of the designated head of the project. He establishes the program by agreement with the individual members as to their particular tasks, and the nature and extent of their participation. He is responsible for seeing that they carry out their functions in accordance with plan, for maintaining communications among them, and for requiring adherence to schedule and budget.

3. **Administration**: Authority to plan and oversee the work is vested in the team leader. Administrative supervisors of the individual members should respect and uphold this authority.
4. **Completion**: The team leader is responsible for the preparation of the final report of findings, conclusions, and recommendations, and for any follow-up that is necessary.

In projects in this category, commitment of the participants to program and schedule is defined by their respective agreements with the team leader. His leadership is established by delegation of authority and his decisions under this authority are controlling.

Projects Under Executive Direction (Type V)

Managers today rely as little as possible on direct assertion of authority and more and more on constructive leadership and suasion. Peter Drucker, in **The Practice of Management** (1954), defines the relationship thus:

"The final function of management is to manage workers and work . . . [This] implies also consideration of the human resource as human beings having, unlike any other resource, personality, citizenship, control over whether they work, how much and how well, and thus requiring motivation, participation, satisfactions, incentives and rewards, leadership, status and function."

When the stage is reached at which a project is to be implemented, however, stronger control is often necessary than that exercised during investigational phases. Earlier the emphasis was on initiative to provide an optimum answer to the problem. Now the required information is available and the thrust is toward putting it to useful purpose as efficiently as possible.

A firm managerial hand, exersised by a senior executive, is called for to make the necessary decisions and to see that they are carried out. Perfectionists among participants at earlier stages often wish to delay matters in the hope that further improvement can be made. The time comes, however, when for the good of the project the specifications must be frozen so that the operation can move smoothly ahead.

Bearing in mind that a good executive will exert his authority with discretion, he is nevertheless in control. His plans require fixed commitments on a program and schedule from all specialized groups which are involved. His leadership is autocratic if he needs to exercise it in this manner. His authority is vested through delegation to him by the management.

Introduction of Interdisciplinary Techniques into Large Meetings

Large meetings are rarely able to come to grips efficiently with specific problems because they are a forum for widely differing opinions, but such assemblies have an important role as a democratic process to promote exchange of views and to encourage future collaboration. A major hindrance is the lack of precise definitions of the issues to insure channeling of the debate toward essentials.

In this section, three devices are described for promoting more efficient action. All of them are interdisciplinary in the sense of affording a medium for the integration of varying opinions. The procedures are: (1) convening the assembly as a committee of the whole to reach consensus without formal commitment; (2) interspersing small working groups among general presentations; and (3) focusing attention on specific subjects by means of a small panel of judges to rule on the relevance of the discussion.

Informal Consensus of a Committee of the Whole. A skillful chairman, adopting the parliamentary procedure of convening the assembly as a committee of the whole (a device rarely used by non-legal bodies), can lead the meeting effectively into establishing the basis for later formal action. By requesting an informal show of hands on an orderly succession of issues, he can guide the participants toward a systematic framework of agreement. The fact that the opinions are not binding, because of another opportunity later on for formal voting, reduces the bitter-end confrontations that so often prolong discussions. If the consensus on a point is the expression of a strong majority, the participants themselves will help to police long-winded contrary arguments. If the division seems to be about equal, a task force of opponents and neutrals can be appointed to report back with some acceptable compromises.

To illustrate, this procedure has been used in a professional group of several hundred members, to lay the basis for a completely revised constitution. Formal approval of its wording at later meetings, of course, aroused the usual heated debate, but reference to the informal polls on many questions helped to confine arguments to reasonable length.

Interdisciplinary Categories

Mixing Small Working Groups with General Meetings. This procedure has been adopted by quite a number of organizations which have become dissatisfied with the results of programs made up only of formal papers or talks by invited speakers, followed by the usual desultory discussion. If the participants decide that they would like to stimulate more positive action from their assemblies, they turn to the use of working groups, preferably of not more than four to 10 members, in the hope that they will interact effectively.

This style of meeting was used very successfully, for instance, in a three-week training course for 38 Egyptian technical managers held in Cairo, U.A.R., in 1964, the first of its kind ever organized in a developing country. It was sponsored by the Egyptian National Institute of Management Development (NIMD), which selected the participants, and was financed by the Ford Foundation. The formal presentations were made by a four-man team from the Arthur D. Little organization, of which I was the leader, plus several local lecturers on special subjects. To provide teaching aids for the meeting, I wrote a 35,000 word syllabus (later published in revised form as **Management of Technical Programs,** Praeger, 1965); this was given to the participants on arrival together with copies of over 20 selected original publications.

The lectures and discussions averaged somewhat over an hour in length and were alternated with longer sessions of four working groups of 8-10 members each, selected to give representation to government employees, industry, and public enterprises. After an introductory meeting, each group elected a chairman and a secretary, with a discrete advisor from the presentation team. Each group was asked to select one or more projects pertinent to the local economy, to prepare a technoeconomic justification, to outline a program of investigation, to propose an interdisciplinary team structure, and to make rough estimates of time required, cost of the investigation, and cost of a commercial plant (on the last point considerable latitude was, of course, permissible because there was not time to consult a reference library). A pair of representatives from each team made a presentation to the entire audience and defended its conclusions against criticism from the floor. By the end of the course, the small groups were working well together and had proposed several useful projects.

Use of a Jury to Control Discussion. At a two-week symposium on the management of research and development in Medellín, Colombia in 1969, the attendance consisted of 40 representatives of universities and institutions, but only a few from industry. The organizers had arranged a diversified program with a long list of speakers, a number of whom attended for only a day or two. The sponsors hoped that suggestions for projects would arise spontaneously out of the discussions. Even when five small working groups were used in addition, with an advisor, they did not prove very successful because of lack of time.

I was to speak on the systematic programming of research on the third afternoon and fourth morning. From earlier visits to all the working groups, it was apparent to me that little was happening except general discussions without focus on specific ideas. In a search for means of instilling a sense of purpose into the program, I hit on the scheme of a small jury to channel the proceedings by soliciting project suggestions from the entire audience, selecting the most promising, and then judging their merits from short presentations by their sponsors. I announced this plan at the beginning of my talk, found that it appealed to the audience, and thereafter interspersed jury activities at intervals during my presentation and later. The object was, of course, to prod the working groups into positive action.

A jury of an economist, an engineer, and a technologist was elected by the assembly with my guidance. In spite of exhortation to produce suggestions, only a few were serious enough to arouse much interest. These subjects were: (1) an engineering analysis of losses in agricultural products between farm and consumer; (2) a comprehensive survey of the professional activities of technically trained personnel in Colombia; and (3) a program for providing technical information and service to small firms. (Some additional work on these proposals has subsequently been carried out by local organizations.) It would have helped greatly to start the activity earlier in the conference and to keep the jury active in interspersed sessions throughout the program.

In summary, the idea of a jury was a good one for arousing the interest of the audience in systematic project selection, although the time was too short to get the full benefit. The procedure would be effective in a group of 100 or more people.

CHAPTER THREE
TASK FORCES FOR NEW PRODUCT DEVELOPMENT

As a practical example of the organization and management of a task force, this initial discussion uses a case for the development of a new product, a subject which has advantages for the purpose. First, the end result is in the tangible form of a physical object. Second, a range of distinct technical disciplines is obviously called for. Third, the merits of the methodology have been proved by successful use by many organizations. Finally, the course of development from concept to commercial scale can be divided into several stages which illustrate the use of a succession of interlocking teams, as described in Chapter Four. The present chapter deals with the first, small-scale stage to characterize the product by a prototype made in the laboratory or model shop.

The most effective task forces for product development are "Oriented Structured Teams with Constraints," classified as Type IV in Chapter Two. The objective can be clearly defined for the successive stages and the range of skills needed for each is readily perceived. The first stage is prototype preparation and evaluation to demonstrate presumptive technical feasibility. Later stages deal with larger scale process development, market research, process confirmation, market confirmation, and comprehensive technoeconomic review, which are covered in detail in the next chapter. This may appear to be an unduly exhaustive program, but for innovative products it is required to reduce the risk of ultimate failure and attendant waste of effort.

For products that are close to present commercial items, and therefore involve less risk, the investigation can be much curtailed. In many such cases, it is even feasible to move directly from small-scale prototype to commercialization, and thus to benefit from more rapid market entry. If the idea turns out to be a failure, the penalty may be less costly than detailed stage-by-stage development. Even in these cases, however, a wise precaution is to carry out a comprehensive technoeconomic review to make sure that important obstacles to success have not been overlooked. This step is advisable because once commercial operation has begun, there is a stubborn resistance to abandonment which may result in a large effort to overcome difficulties that might have been foreseen.

Even successful ideas do not flow smoothly into commercial use after immediate recognition of their merits. Instead, they have to survive a step-by-step assessment from different points of view. A period of at least several weeks is required even in quite simple cases, where the similarity to existing products already on the market can be assumed to provide reliable insights into their chances of success. When they represent a high degree of innovation, with only speculative market potential, several years of work may be necessary before they can be commercialized.

The mortality among concepts for new products is very high. Although data regarding the number of rejections are scanty, some well managed organizations have reported that only a fraction of one percent of all proposed ideas have attained commercial success.

Effective management of research and development programs therefore hinges on systematic procedures for weeding out unlikely projects at an early stage, so that efforts can be concentrated on those that continue to show promise. At the same time, however, the basis for rejection must be tempered by constructive appraisal of the obstacles to success and the probability of overcoming them. Without this safeguard, only the more pedestrian ideas will be accepted and the less certain but more novel concepts, with the potential of technologic breakthroughs, will be eliminated.

Criteria of Feasibility for Products Under Development

Before a project can be safely considered for commercialization, it must meet the requirements of the following six sets of criteria. The progressive depth of their application as more information accumulates in successive stages is shown in Chart II (Chapter Four).

Technical feasibility: can the product be made by procedures that appear to be satisfactory from the technologic point of view?

Manufacturing practicality: when these procedures are examined by production experts, are they acceptable with respect to operating requirements, facilities and equipment, and raw materials?

Marketing potential: is there reasonable expectation of sufficient demand to warrant an operation of economic size?

Regulatory acceptability: does the project pass the tests of legal, regulatory, and public interest restrictions?

Economic justification: do the cost-benefit estimates provide a basis for assuming a successful commercial undertaking?

Enterpreneurial attractiveness: does the concept appeal to the management as a suitable venture?

During the laboratory or model shop stage, these criteria obviously cannot be applied with equal severity. There is not enough information available to permit firm decisions on anything but technical feasibility, which lies within the realm of competence of technologists. Only tentative opinions can be given regarding the other five aspects of feasibility, but it is essential that the concept should be subjected to preliminary examination from these points of view by individuals with the necessary expertise. Otherwise, much work may be wasted by carrying out the perfection of product and process only to find later that there are insurmountable barriers to success.

The situation in an isolated product development group should be considered in contrast with this broader approach. In a highly structured, cellular organization, estimates of practical potential will be based on the views of technologists, who, however competent in their fields, rarely have the necessary backgrounds and expertise to form valid conclusions regarding other commercial requirements. They vigorously apply their talents to making a prototype which in their enthusiasm they assume to be acceptable for production and sale. In a rigid organization, these assumptions may not be challenged by other experts until their program has been completed. As a result, much of the work may have to be done over to meet the new requirements.

The use of interdisciplinary teams for product development is by no means universal. Successful organizations which do not employ the technique are of course mindful of the need to inject other techno-economic skills into the evaluation. This they do by various methods such as periodic project reviews or continuing consulting relationships. I believe, however, that these outside opinions are more acceptable to and more influential on the working group if they come from individuals who are closely identified with the entire project by service as team members; this resistance to outside suggestions is significant enough to have earned the nickname of the "Not Invented Here Syndrome." Further, the time lag in presenting external comments usually causes delay in their consideration and acceptance.

Prerequisites for Task Force Operation

The illustrative example chosen is the idea for an innovative food product. The concept is assumed to arise in the imagination of an experienced technologist in the product development group. From conversations with scientists engaged in long range research, he has learned of new information about the heat stability of certain delicate food constituents. From his acquaintance with improvements in processes for drying sensitive materials at moderate temperatures, the idea occurs to him of combining these two independent items of knowledge to make a cereal product with better nutritive properties and greater convenience in the household. He thus achieves the germ of an invention, but the idea must be reduced to practice if it is to reach utility.

In order to move the concept forward, someone should take charge of the program. The technologist who conceived the idea is a logical choice because of his creative enthusiasm; the research management may, however, for some reason, such as limited availability of his time, entrust the responsibility to one of his colleagues.

Some exploratory work needs to be done to test the soundness of the idea. This may be taken care of by collecting further information from associates or the literature, but often it will require initial laboratory experimentation. Further, there are certain commercial aspects, such as the probable consumer demand and the suitability and the cost of the low temperature drying process for large scale operation. To obtain initial opinions on these points, he needs to consult specialists in market research and process engineering.

These exploratory steps should be monitored by research management to prevent an undue expenditure of effort before the concept is framed as a project for formal review. It is advisable to set some limit on the amount of time that may be spent for this purpose.

The technologist then proceeds to the preparation of a project outline which includes a subject, a statement of the objective, a description of the background, a justification for undertaking the work, an outline of the proposed program, an estimate of manpower requirements and expense, and a target date. A standard form, such as that in Table 3, is often used for this purpose.

The steps involved in organizing and conducting the project can be summarized as follows:

New Product Development

1. Designation of a project leader to carry out exploratory work to round out the project proposal;
2. Preparation of a project outline;
3. Approval of the plan by research management;
4. Organization and indoctrination by the team leader of the other members of the task force regarding the roles they are to play;
5. Coordination by the team leader of all activities and communications within the team, including interim adjustments of program and schedule as warranted by progress of the work;
6. Completion of the task and preparation of the final report;
7. Participation of the team leader and perhaps other members of the group in later stages as the project moves forward toward commercialization.

Selection of Team Leaders

The success of a task force is highly dependent on the ability of the leader to plan the program, to secure the cooperation of a group of specialists, and to co-ordinate their skills to obtain an optimum solution. He is usually selected from the discipline which has the major role in that phase of the problem. He must have professional competence and demonstrated ability as a leader to command the respect of his colleagues. He must have broad understanding and sympathy for the philosophy and methodology of the other disciplines which he has to coordinate.

The style of management of the team leader sets the framework for the operation as a whole. He must respect the integrity of the skills of his co-members. He is not a universal genius, because if he were, no team would be needed but only sets of hands to carry out his instructions. He is a "leader," not a "director" or "manager." If he is too domineering, he will fail to maintain an atmosphere of creative participation. If he is too lenient in permitting deviations from plan, progress will be delayed.

The team leader must be adroit in setting up a communications system within the group. Information must be distributed on a need-to-know basis, so that each member will have enough knowledge of the trend of the findings of his colleagues to adjust his own program, without being deluged with details which are not pertinent to his work.

Communications should include both written reports of information that needs to be digested and group meetings to reach consensus on the future program.

Table 3
Form of Project Outline

Subject: a short title for easy reference.

Object: a concise statement of the concept.

Background: a summary of information on which technical feasibility is based.

Justification: a rough forecast of utility, market, and manufacturing practicality.

Program: a tentative outline of the proposed method of investigation.

Personnel: a preliminary list of individuals representing different disciplines, together with an estimate of the amount of time required from each.

Cost: translation of team composition into a budget, plus any other major items of expense.

Schedule: proposed completion date.

Future Work: a projection of supplementary work in later stages.

Project Leader: signature and date.

Approval: signature and date.

The team leader is responsible for preparing the outline of his program to submit to research management for approval. If he is not given adequate authority to define the problem, plan the program, and oversee the work, it is illogical and unfair to hold him responsible for the results. To supply the required information he needs to do additional exploratory analysis and work to define the responsibility which he is accepting on behalf of his colleagues as well as himself. If he is wise, he will collect advice from various sources, particularly from representatives of other participating disciplines, without which he may

New Product Development 29

flounder in projecting the roles they are to play. It is obviously better to consider the views of prospective team members before locking them into a defined program which they will later find unsatisfactory.

Planning the Interdisciplinary Team

During the preparation of the project outline, the composition of the task force begins to take form in the team leader's thinking. For effective operation the team is best broken up into two parts: (1) a small key group of three to not more than five or six members representing those disciplines believed to be most significant for solving the problem; (2) a second group whose contributions are important, but more easily set up as separate inputs which can be incorporated into the planning and assessment of the total program by the key team.

The requirements for team composition can be reached in various depths, ranging from an elaborate net-work analysis to a simple intuitive selection process at the hands of a veteran team leader who can base his selection on experiences in the successful handling of previous tasks of similar nature. The choice will be influenced also by the breadth of expertise represented by other team members whose participation he expects to secure; if there are several whom he knows to have versatile capabilities, he can count on them to handle certain aspects for which he might otherwise require additional team members.

As a first step, the team leader may use a preliminary tabulation as in Table 4 of the requisite inputs of knowledge or opinions. In this form it can be used for checking the completeness of the array of skills, particularly for discussions with R & D management, prospective team members, and other departments in the organization.

The team leader must then prepare a more detailed breakdown of the schedule for team participation. This is necessary to check further the array of expertise, to inform prospective team members of the effort and timing expected from each, and to confirm the budget for the entire program for which he is responsible. The end result is shown in tabular form in Table 5.

This team structure has purposely been made quite elaborate to illustrate the range of skills which may be needed. It may appear to be overly complex to managers who are unfamiliar with task forces. Nonetheless, it is typical of teams used in sophisticated organizations, although the estimates of schedules are more detailed than that used in

Table 4
COMPOSITION OF A TASK FORCE TO DEVELOP A NOVEL CEREAL PRODUCT

Group or Skill	Individual	Function
Key Team		
Team Leader Product Development	Tim Upman	Planning, coordination and control of entire program, supervision of product formulation
Flavor Panel	Gus Tibus (plus 3 other panel members)	Evaluation of eating quality and forecast of consumer acceptance
Market Research	Sherlock Homes	Study of market potential, competition, pricing, preliminary consumer tests
Process Engineering	Ernest Mason	Advisor on process feasibility, initial estimates of manufacturing costs
Other Major Participants		
Product Development	Abel Halper	Formulation of product
Product Development	Loyal Ade	Preparation of samples
Experimental Kitchen	Patience Cooke	Practical testing of product
Analytical Methods	Marc Wright	Analytical and quality control methods, specifications
Operations Research	Sterling Worth	Design of experiments
Advisors on Special Problems, Flexible Schedules		
Physical Chemistry	Stark Mesure	Consultation on physical properties
Carbohydrate Chemistry	LeBel Sweet	Consultation on raw materials
Protein Chemistry	Twining Amin	Consultation on behavior of constituents
Colloid Chemistry	Polly State	Consultation on process effects
Nutrition	Constance Diette	Consultation on dietary values
Packaging	Tate Wrappin	Initial concepts for containers

many cases. It is to be understood that the proposed amounts of time are subject to modification in the light of findings during the course of the work.

An estimated cost of $80,000 for this stage of the project given in Table 5 is based on an average cost of $250.00 per technical man-day, an estimate that is supported by the experience of many research laboratories in the United States. To reach a figure of total expenditure by R & D, we may allow $60,000 more for Process Development in pilot plant runs, and $40,000 for the cost of preparing samples and conducting field consumer tests. This gives a total of $180,000 for research and development, which may well represent less than 10 percent of the total cost of implementing the project on commercial scale. A figure of several million dollars for launching an innovative new product is not out of line with acceptable experience.

To complete a table of skills distribution as illustrated in Table 5 the team leader needs to settle with each prospective member the particular part of the program for which he will be responsible. This involves definition of the form and substance of the contribution to be made, the amount of effort, the timing, the possible changes that may be required, the reporting schedule, etc. Agreement must be reached between the team leader and the respective participant on all these points.

Each team member should secure the tacit or formal approval of his administrative superior for this tentative commitment of his time during the course of the project. In well-established systems for interdisciplinary task forces, this approval can be smoothly arranged. In more rigid organization structures, explanation and formal approval may be necessary.

It is frequently the case that only the R & D and Engineering Departments will have a highly organized time distribution system, while the rest of the company operates on an ad hoc schedule by responding to pressure for use of the skills of each group or department. Just to make sure that heads of these departments receive advance notice of planned calls for their assistance, it is obligatory to discuss the requirements in advance.

Use of Operations Research Techniques. The use of the skills of OR specialists in interdisciplinary teams is a constructive policy. They are particularly helpful in identifying variables and their interrela-

Table 5
DISTRIBUTION OF SKILLS IN A TASK FORCE

Group or Skill	Estimate of Man-Days						Total
Key Team	J	F	M	A	M	J	
Team Leader							
Product Development	8	8	8	10	12	12	58
Flavor Panel	2	2	4	6	6	4	24
Market Research	3	2	1	3	4	2	15
Process Engineering	1	1	2	2	3	3	12
						Subtotal	109
Other Major Participants							
Product Development	4	8	8	12	15	12	59
Product Development	6	12	15	18	18	10	79
Experimental Kitchen	-	4	2	4	5	3	18
Analytical Methods	2	1	2	4	5	3	17
Operations Research	3	1	1	-	3	3	11
						Subtotal	184
Advisors on Special Problems, Flexible Schedules							
Physical Chemistry							5
Carbohydrate Chemistry							6
Protein Chemistry							8
Colloid Chemistry							4
Nutrition							4
Packaging							4
						Subtotal	31
						Grand Total	324

tionships. They provide valuable guidance for the design of investigational approaches.

The concept of operations research achieved prominence during World War II as a procedure for logical analysis of complex military operations. The function was carried out by teams recruited from mathematics, the physical sciences, and other disciplines. Its interdisciplinary character was striking because the practitioners were transfers or transplants from other specialized fields, and this feature was emphasized by some of the early leaders.

The view that OR is the source of interdisciplinology is not in accord with the opinion of John F. Magee (President of Arthur D. Little, Inc., private communication), and the author. Magee says, "ADL has practiced interdisciplinary team research long before the term 'OR' was articulated. To me, the essence of OR is not the interdisciplinary nature; quite the contrary. It is the application of the processes of the experimental sciences to the subject of real, purposeful and organized human activities—'operations.'

"Over the course of the last 20 years, OR has increasingly assumed the character of a discipline: a professional society, a growing body of method, academic curricula and degrees, and a sense of identity. We try to incorporate OR as one of the disciplines in traditional ADL interdisciplinary teams."

Approval of Project Program. It is usual practice in research departments to have formal procedures for the appoval of projects. These provide a means for the responsible executives to check plans and justification, to decide priorities with respect to other activities, and to make any necessary adjustments in manpower allocations or financial budgets to accommodate the new work.

Once management has approved the outline, they delegate responsibility for the carrying out of the program to the team leader. While they will continue to exert general—but not detailed—overseeing of progress, their functions are to assist by exerting administrative authority in overcoming operating problems, particularly when these arise in relations with other parts of the organization, and to consider sympathetically major changes in program arising from the course of the investigation. Their dealings with team members will be through the leader, and not with individuals except as he may agree, in order that his authority and prestige may be maintained.

Organization of the Team

As soon as the project has been approved, the team leader needs to confirm with individual members the nature of their participation, securing the consent of their administrative superiors directly through personal contact, or indirectly through proper notification by the participants of those responsible for their schedules of activity. Each team member should be given appropriate indoctrination; this is often provided by an initial team meeting, so that all will become familiar with the total program. Each should be provided with a copy of the approved project outline, should have his particular assignment confirmed by agreement with the team leader, and should be given instructions regarding communication procedures. He should be given warning of any required flexibility in his commitment, so that he can provide accommodations in his schedule.

Team Activities

The team leader has a vital role in keeping in touch with the work being carried out by each member. He may need to exert pressure on some to make sure that their activities are in harmony with the plan and schedule, and should refer as frequently as necessary to the approved project outline and any supplementary agreements. He may need to assist them in overcoming obstacles, either technical or administrative. In some cases, he may need to alter assignments in the light of progress of the work as a whole.

The leader must watch carefully the effectiveness of the communication system. He must make sure that important new information is transmitted promptly to others whose activities may be affected. He must see that team meetings are arranged with sufficient frequency and depth, and that written material is suitably distributed. He can often reduce the effort required to prepare a final report by suitable arrangements for the form and substance of interim reports. He should pay attention to information requirements of other parts of the company.

The leader must be particularly alert for major breakthroughs or obstacles that can affect the team program markedly. He must keep the management of R & D informed of any impending major changes in activities, and should promptly submit a revised project outline for approval whenever necessary.

New Product Development

Reporting on Completion of the Project

The team leader is responsible for the preparation of the final report or reports, including recommendations for further work to carry the project forward toward commercial application, although the framing of the project outlines for these additional stages and the responsibility for team leadership is often entrusted to others. The expenditure of effort on reporting may amount to as much as 10 per cent of the total technical man-hours allocated to the project; when budgetary control is practiced, allowance should be made for this cost in the original project estimate.

Although some team leaders may prefer to prepare the final report themselves, it is preferable to lay out in advance a program for reporting by each major participant. In addition to saving time, this procedure ensures that the wording will be that of those who have done the work, thus avoiding inadvertent changes in meaning or emphasis that may arise when the writing is done by some one else. It also gives the other team members a fuller sense of responsibility in participation.

Continuing Activities in Later Stages

To secure continuing flow of information and know-how from stage to stage, the team leader and other selected members should be included in teams formed to carry out additional development work on the route to commercialization, as discussed in Chapter Four. This provides effective liaison with the group responsible for earlier phases, and also insures their interest in the entire sequence, so that they are alert to the value of new information that may accrue in their respective spheres of specialization.

This is a very important function, not only for the particular project, but also to promote a sense of solidarity in the organization as a whole. All too often in cellular structures personnel involved in earlier work lose contact with later progress to such an extent that they do not derive the stimulus of having made a personal contribution to a commercially successful venture. This sometimes results in a feeling of neglect as forgotten men in the complex of activities which leads to the agressive posture of the company.

Co-ordination of Long-Range Research with Applied Projects

Coupling between science and technology has until quite recently been a chancy occurrence—a passive reliance on serendipity. As the opportunities have become recognized, and as expenditures for basic research have increased greatly, more and more attention has been given to trying to make the linkage less haphazard.

The relationship between fundamental and long-range research and its application to practical problems has been the subject of much argument. Indeed, even the definitions are in dispute; some claim that the distinction between basic and applied work is a matter of the purity of the motives of the researcher. Hence the validity of statistics based on such clouded definitions is open to some questions, including those cited below, but certain it is that they have enough consistency to reveal trends.

Many researchers in pure science spurn the idea of utility. Others, particularly to win support for their projects, make rosy prophecies for the utility of their work.

Fundamental research, aimed at uncovering new knowledge, is carried out chiefly in universities and in institutions set up for the purpose. Government agencies and private industry also conduct or support work of this type, but often prefer to call it "oriented basic research." There is sound logic for this activity. Innovative applied projects usually require two to five or more years for fruition. Beyond that period, before one can foresee clearly the technology that will develop, there is definite need to stimulate new scientific knowledge in selected areas to provide the underpinning for future investigations.

Data on the size of the basic research effort have been released by the National Science Foundation in "National Patterns of R & D Resources: Funds & Manpower in the United States 1953-1973." According to this survey, total expenditure for basic research in 1973 is estimated at $4.5 billion, 15 percent of total R & D spending as compared with 9 percent in 1953; during the decade 1963-73 the basic research share increased nearly 50 percent, an average annual change of plus 5 percent. In 1973 the Federal Government is to finance about 58 percent of total basic research, almost the same share as in 1971 and 1972, with five agencies accounting for 88 percent. During the decade 1960-70 the total number of R & D scientists, excluding engineers, engaged in basic research showed little change; in 1970 about 45 percent of doctorate degree holders and 25 percent of nondoctorates were in basic research activities.

In a study of "Scientific Research and Innovation" Price and Bass (**Science, 164,** 802, 1969) conclude that usually there is no direct path between new science and potential application. The linkage is improved by "coupling," which in 38 of 244 cases surveyed was indirect, while 88 were attributed to the use of published information without intervention of the authors, 96 to direct coordination, and 28 to the influence of a "gatekeeper" or "product champion." For the good of the cause, much more attention should be paid to the mechanism of coupling.

University Activities. Universities and colleges are the primary performers of basic research in the U.S. According to the NSF survey, they are expected to carry out 58 percent of the total in 1973, with little change from the preceding year. During 1953-73 they increased their share from 35 to 58 percent.

Non-profit institutions, which devote about one-half their R & D funds to basic research, are expected to support 5 percent of the U.S. total in 1973, as compared with 7 percent in 1953.

Government Programs. I am much impressed with the systematic procedures developed by the Air Force Office of Scientific Research for planning its program of support for outside projects; it does not operate its own laboratories. The Army Research Office and the Office of Naval Research use similar policies in their efforts to provide basic knowledge for long-range military needs.

AFOSR has adopted the philosophy of "colonizing," by clusters of projects, those scientific areas deemed most important for future technology which are not now being adequately stressed. For this purpose its staff of 31 civilian scientists and 23 officers with technical backgrounds, using the services of outside advisory panels, employs matrix analysis to select program elements. It is collaborating intimately with other Air Force and Department of Defense organizations, including planning agencies, other scientific laboratories, development laboratories, operational functions, and suppliers of hardware. It is applying interdisciplinary principles to its internal programming and to its contacts with others; each project manager has two functions: monitoring developments in the specific area of science and participating in a multidisciplinary attack on applied problems. Providing opportunities for younger scientists to develop their talents is an important objective. AFOSR is supporting about 600 projects in which roughly 2,000 scientists are engaged. Its budget for FY 1974 is about $30,000,000, including 7 percent for internal operating costs.

Industrial Activities. In **Basic Research in the Navy** (Vol. I, p. 56, 1959, an Arthur D. Little report to the Naval Research Advisory Committee), a survey of 33 leading companies, representing one-fifth of the Nation's and one-half of industry's total basic research funds, revealed that on the average they were devoting at that time about 10 percent of their R & D budgets to long-range projects, some to the extent of 20 percent of such expenditures. Since that time there has been some disillusionment with the merits of these activities, in my opinion because of insufficient attention to the mechanism of coupling. According to the NSF survey, in 1973 industry is expected to finance 14 percent of the country's basic research, a drop of more than half from the 30 percent in 1953. The current level accounts for about 5 percent of total R & D funds in industry.

Comment. An obvious means of improving the coupling between basic researchers and applied work is to encourage their participation in task forces formed to carry out projects aimed at definite goals. As a practical measure, they might devote 5-10 percent of their time to such activities. This would permit them to apply their talents as advisers on the use of advanced scientific knowledge for concrete objectives, and at the same time sharpen their perception of opportunities to shape their long-range programs toward increased potential relevance. It would help to break down the barriers between their somewhat isolated environment and the mainstream of the programs of their organizations. This should improve the morale of both scientists and technologists.

CHAPTER FOUR
TASK FORCES FOR SUCCESSIVE STAGES

If the full benefits of interdisciplinary procedures are to be obtained, the principles used in the prototype stage of product development, described in the previous chapter, should be extended to the succession of activities leading to commercialization. This ensures company-wide participation. As the project moves forward to practical fulfillment, a sequence of task forces with different mixtures of skills is required. New information permits more rigorous application of the criteria of feasibility. The frames of reference become more and more positive as guidelines.

Coordination of Successive Project Teams

To ensure a smooth succession of interdisciplinary teams, designation of a coordinator with adequate authority, prestige, and personal involvement is desirable. This function may not be needed until the project has passed through two additional evaluation stages, namely, process development and market research. If the concept has sufficient momentum because of the enthusiasm of research managers, these smaller scale and less expensive stages may be undertaken under their supervision.

When the more costly stages of process and market confirmation are reached, however, it is highly important that the backing of top management be secured through this coordinator. He can insist on thorough evaluation at the end of each stage before further work is undertaken. He can enlist the participation of other departments and groups in the company in assessing feasibility before they become directly involved. He can ensure proper feed-back and feed-forward of pertinent information.

This coordinator may be selected from various parts of the company provided he has the necessary breadth and forcefulness. He may be the team leader of one of the task forces. He may be a general executive. Above all, he must have the confidence of top management and must perform under their aegis.

Progressive Application of Criteria of Feasibility

As the project moves forward by stages, evaluation of its merits can be conducted with increasing severity. In Chart II the progressive depth of assessment is summarized. In Chart III and the accompanying discussion, the composition of successive task forces is indicated.

The progressive procedures involve an approach which mobilizes the necessary skills on a company-wide basis. They encourage an effective feed-back of findings to obtain additional pertinent information from those who have been active in earlier stages. They promote feed-forward of the status of the investigations to bring out the views of those who will later on have responsibility for larger scale, more costly phases.

The major purpose is to disclose obstacles to success at an early date. The work must be directed toward overcoming these difficulties, or, if they appear to be unsurmountable at the time, to avoid wasted effort by abandoning or postponing the investigation.

Exploratory Phase. The objective of the preliminary study is to reduce the concept to a workable basis for planning product development. The idea is not yet sufficiently defined to permit more than a general opinion of product and process feasibility.

Product Development. At the end of this initial technologic stage, the availability of a prototype justifies preliminary opinions regarding the acceptability of product, process, and raw material requirements. The definition of product characteristics and performance permits an initial check on whether it fits with growth policies of the management. A very rough estimate of production cost and volume of sales can be made, often by rule-of-thumb; the greater the novelty of the product, the greater the uncertainty in these figures. Initial views can be expressed on the patent and regulatory situation.

Process Development. Process development work is usually done on quite small scale. This step may be omitted when the product is closely related to current operations of the company. Initial evaluation of the process requires examination of the procedures by engineers on a larger scale in the laboratory or pre-pilot plant. Results of the work often indicate that the initial specifications of the product have to be modified to suit the characteristics of the process. Earlier work was often carried out with refined starting materials or components and with a high degree of technical supervision, so that the requirements have to be examined in terms of conventional raw materials and operating control. The process flow diagram provides a

CHART II
PROGRESSIVE APPLICATION OF TECHNO-ECONOMIC CRITERIA

CRITERIA / STAGES	Product	Process	Marketing	Managerial Interest	Raw Materials	Facilities	Manufacturing	Cost-Benefit	Legal Aspects
Product Concept	General description	Probably feasible	Probably salable	*EXPLORATORY STAGE*					
Product Development	Initial prototype	Preliminary appraisal	Preliminary approach	Conformance with plans	Preliminary selection			Preliminary estimate	Initial review
Process Development	Possible modification	Basic design			Preliminary specifications	Initial concept	Feasibility review	Revised estimate	Preliminary review
Market Projection	Performance evaluation	Reliability review	Specific opportunities	Confirmation of interest				Revised estimate	
Process Confirmation	Possible modification	Final design	Acceptability of product	*CONFIRMATION STAGES* Review of specifications	Complete flow diagram	Confirmation of practicality	Semi-final estimates	Interim approval
Market Confirmation	Firm specifications		Confirmed opportunities	Critical review				Semi-final estimates	
Comprensive Review	Final specifications	Confirmed design	Marketing plan	Coordination	Firm specifications	Final design	Manufacturing plan	Final estimates	Final approval
Management Action				*IMPLEMENTATION STAGES* DECISION TO COMMERCIALIZE					
Manufacturing Mobilization	Consultation	Consultation	Information	General supervision	Procurement	Construction	Primary responsibility	Financing and costing	Patents Licenses
Marketing Mobilization	Consulation	Consulation	Primary responsibility	General supervision	Information	Information	Scheduling	Costing	Contracts
Commercial Operation	Improvements	Improvements	Sales operations	Overseeing	Purchasing control	Adjustment	Plant operation	Cost control	Continuing review

basis for an initial concept of facilities and manufacturing procedures, as well as for a revised estimate of operating costs and plant investment. A more searching examination of legal restrictions is advisable.

Market Estimation. While preliminary opinions on market potential were required as background for the product development work, these cannot be critically reviewed until the prototype has been produced by an acceptable process. Then, too, the evaluation of performance by laboratory testing needs to be rechecked by methods which preferably approach actual conditions of use by customers. Also a more careful study of competing products must be carried out to define the merits of the product in the marketplace.

Different types of market analysis are required for industrial and consumer products. For the former, samples are submitted to representative potential customers for laboratory and small plant trials. For the latter, consumer tests are carried out with representative juries. Obviously, sizable quantities of samples are required in either case, and because the cost of preparing them represents considerable expense, their volume and representative character should be carefully regulated.

At the end of this stage, specific marketing opportunities can be identified and characterized. The conclusions of the market research group should be checked with the sales department and with general management to confirm their opinions that the project should be continued. The information permits firmer estimates of sales volume and pricing and also contributes to the knowledge of marketing channels and trade practices.

Process Confirmation. This stage is carried out by development engineers on pilot plant or semicommercial scale. The cost of installing and operating a complete pilot plant is high, and the necessity for this expense should be carefully analyzed. It may be possible to schedule trial runs on existing commercial equipment. On it may be feasible to confine new equipment and processing to certain steps, and to complete the rest of the operation in available facilities. Emphasis should be placed on using commercial raw materials and operating controls so that the product may be as representative as possible of its ultimate specifications. Pilot plant operations may also be necessary to produce the large samples required for market confirmation.

Market Confirmation. Positive evidence of the existence of demand by customers is best obtained by test marketing. For industrial products, this proof is made definite by negotiation of sales contracts, although the commitment may be contingent on the final decision of the management to authorize commercialization. For consumer products, they may be offered for sale in a few selected retail outlets or areas.

To encourage demand, the products usually have to bear prices representative of those planned when the project has attained commercial scale. The cost of production in a pilot plant is almost certain to be much higher, because the operation will be below minimum economic size and also because the overhead due to an abnormal degree of technical supervision to obtain data and experience will be expensive. When the production of large quantities to meet customer demand arises, cost-benefit should be carefully studied to avoid excessive expense at this stage unless rapid entry into the market is very desirable for competitive reasons. In general, any attempt to market products from pilot operations will show a large deficit, if the costs are ascertained in the same manner that would be used for commercial scale.

Comprehensive Review. A very important precaution at the end of these confirmation steps is to carry out an appraisal of the merits of the project by all those specialists who have been engaged in it throughout its course. When a review of this kind is omitted, the penalty may be very severe. New technologic or economic factors may have arisen which will invalidate the basic premises on which the successive investigations were carried out. Even when a well-managed series of task forces has been used, with a good warning system for unforeseen developments, an orderly assessment for the entire project is highly desirable. Each participating group should be called on to reaffirm its conclusions.

The necessity for a comprehensive review is demonstrated by the following case history. During the course of a diversification study, the president of the client company asked our team to "take a quick look" at an appropriation request for three-quarters of a million dollars for a unit to make a new product. The request had been signed by seven department executives. The justification was based on a market projection made two years earlier, in which one customer was expected to buy over one-half the proposed production. The "quick

CHART III

REPRESENTATION OF DISCIPLINES IN SUCCESSIVE TASK FORCES

KEY: ★Team Leadership   +Team Membership   ●Consultation   ○Information

DEVELOPMENT STAGES / FUNCTIONAL GROUPS	Applied Research	Process Engineering	Market Research	Engineering Development	Marketing	Management	Manufacturing	General Engineering	Purchasing	Finance and Accounting	Legal and Patents
PREPARATORY STAGES											
PRODUCT DEVELOPMENT	★	+	+								○
PROCESS DEVELOPMENT	+	★	●	+	○	○	●		○		
MARKET ESTIMATION	+	+	★		+	○				○	
CONFIRMATION STAGES											
PROCESS CONFIRMATION	+	+	○	★	○	○	+	+	○	●	●
MARKET CONFIRMATION	●	●	+	+	★	●	○	○	○	○	+
COMPREHENSIVE REVIEW	●	●	●	●	+	★	+	+	●	+	●
DECISION TO COMMERCIALIZE						★					
MOBILIZATION OF RESOURCES	○	○	○	○	★	★★	★	★	★	+	+

Sequential Task Forces   47

look" required less than two hours; it had been announced in the trade press a short time before that this major customer had merged with a competing firm which was already making products closely related to the proposed intermediate. Without this volume, the new facility would have been much below minimum economic size. In the face of this obstacle, the client executives all agreed that their approval had been premature.

Management Action. When all this information has been made available to the management, there are certain to be gaps in factual knowledge which must be taken into account before the final decision to commercialize is reached. The chief executives must consider the undertaking in terms of their short- and long-range goals for development of the company, and for this purpose written policies are often used to establish guidelines. They must consider the project in the perspective of alternative uses of resources. They must weigh its relationship to the pattern of other commitments they have made or plan to make. They must review their opinions of probable trends in the general economy in which the project would have to compete.

The decision is a heavy responsibility. The succession of task forces should strive to make available the maximum of factual information and valid opinions to reduce the inherent uncertainties. An adverse decision at this late stage causes not only an unfortunate wastage of effort but also a blow to the morale of all the participants. These considerations emphasize the necessity for management to apply critical judgment at interim steps, preferably by making a clear statement of guidelines for the application of technoeconomic criteria. When managers decide to abandon a project, the reasons should be transmitted to the team members to exemplify their attitudes toward desirable characteristics of new projects, and also to clarify their own decision-making processes.

Manufacturing and Marketing Mobilization. When the decision is reached to implement the project, further participation by members of the succession of task forces should be required. While primary responsibility for putting plans into operation rests on manufacturing and marketing executives, who should of course be in close harmony, the coordination of all other expertise which can contribute to a successful outcome is needed. This not only aids the solution of practical problems but also contributes to the morale of the entire company.

Types of Responsibilities in Successive Task Forces

The coordinative relationships among different corporate functions at successive stages are codified in Chart III. This tabulation makes use of four types of involvement which are discussed below: (a) team leadership; (b) team participation; (c) consultative relationship; and (d) information requirement. These are all reflected in the planning, organization, and operation of task force activities.

The basic principles of the chart should need little explanation, except for discussion of the types of participation which are summarized below. It illustrates the fact that, as the project moves toward commercialization from one major stage to another, there are successive changes in team objectives, leadership, and composition. There is a corresponding increase in intensity of application of the sets of criteria shown in Chart II. As information is accumulated, it becomes appropriate to examine in more detail the commercial aspects which are prerequisite to the final decision by management to implement the findings.

The next to last stage—Comprehensive Review—is one that is very necessary to avoid costly failures. All the functions that have been involved in the series of studies should be called upon to confirm their earlier feasibility statements. After all, several years may have elapsed, especially in the case of innovative products, since the original work was done. New scientific discoveries may have rendered the product or process specifications partially or largely questionable. Changes in the market place may have occurred through the introduction of improved competitive products. New patents or regulations may exert restrictive influences. Inflationary trends, which have not been fully taken into account in earlier calculations, or other changes in the economic climate, may introduce hazards to commercial success. Even the internal situation in the company, such as other commitments which have been made, may have altered the premises on which previous evaluations were based. Prudent management demands that an up-to-date review of all pertinent factors should be carried out before final decision is reached.

Team Leadership. The functions of team leaders have been discussed above. They include planning and overseeing the operation of the task force, and coordinating the findings of the diversified inputs into a report which serves as the basis for decision as to future course of action. Usually a major part of the work of each stage lies within the discipline of the team leader.

Active Participation. The nature of the responsibility at each stage requires considerable additional effort from both the administrative group or discipline to which the team leader belongs and also from other parts of the organization. The authority of the leader over members of his own group, insofar as their participation in the task force is concerned, is implicit in his appointment to this responsibility and in approval of the project proposal, including a manpower table, which he has prepared; this authority may, of course, be confirmed formally. The members from other administrative groups should be subject to the same responsibility for carrying out his plan, but because he is unlikely to have equal expertise in their special skills, they will have more latitude in the use of their talents; hence, though there is no routine channel of his authority, his general supervision over their technical activities on the project must be recognized both by them and by their administrative supervisors.

Consultative Responsibility. In this capacity, some members of the team are called on for comment and criticism, rather than for detailed work. Their function is to keep generally informed of progress, and to interject information and opinion whenever suitable on the basis of their specialized backgrounds. The schedules for participation are more flexible and less demanding than those of members who are playing a continuing active role, but the authority of the team leader to require their services must be recognized in the same spirit.

Information Requirement. The fourth type of involvement is still less direct, but nevertheless very important for the comprehensive evaluation of the work. While the two purposes are mentioned separately, both of them usually apply to the same group. On the one hand, it serves to alert other functions in the organization to questions on which they feel they should inject information or opinion. On the other, it gives advance notice to departments or functions which will be directly involved later on so that they may prepare themselves to assume these responsibilities.

Participants in this category should be kept informed in a general way, without full details unless they request them. This permits them to raise questions or give warnings at their option. These responsibilities do not carry the implication of formal approval, a process which would impede progress, but it places them on notice that they should take action whenever they feel it to be advisable. Top management, for example, has of course the prerogative of raising issues at any time, but at certain critical stages their active consideration of the status of the project is required to confirm that it still is in accordance with corporate objectives and plans. Similarly, the legal staff should point out pertinent changes in regulations or the patent situation. Finally, at later stages key participants in earlier phases should be kept informed so that they can supply information which may have become available since they were more directly involved.

To summarize, the chart is a condensed check-list to illustrate the broad character of company-wide participation in new product development. Many organizations use much more detailed compilations of critical decision points, as many as 100 or more, within the broad categories of activities which are shown. It has the aim of describing major action steps and omits the procedures for managerial or committee approval; for example, consideration of a large investment in pilot plant facilities would surely go at least to top management for approval and would probably involve action by the Board of Directors.

System of Stages and Steps in Product Development

The detailed list of stages and steps which immediately follows should be valuable as a check list to make sure that no essential points have been overlooked in final preparation for the commercialization of a new product. It may appear to have formidable length. Certainly short-cuts can be used in the case of items that are closely related to the present product line; here the back-ground of experience gives assurance that market entry should not pose undue hazards. Further, in the case of small organizations, in which relations between functional corporate groups are close, any gaps have probably been closed through intimate internal discussions. Nevertheless, it is not amiss in either case to spend a reasonable time going down the list as a precaution against oversight.

There is also quite a bit of seeming repetition of matters treated earlier in the chapter. The advantage of having a complete check list in convenient form, however, compensates for this objection.

The list had an interesting origin. Many years ago I found myself

Sequential Task Forces

chairman of a workshop on management of research under the auspices of the American Management Association. There were more than a score of very experienced technical directors from sizable companies, about evenly divided between the process industries and the electromechanical industries. As discussion leader I was not content to waste such an excellent collection of talent in hackneyed topics that so often make up the subject matter of this type of meeting. I suggested to the group a detailed breakdown of all the activities that go into the commerialization of an innovative new product, and the proposal was enthusiastically received.

We started with the process industries, using a volunteer at the blackboard to write down the steps as they were proposed by individual members, grouped under the major stages in development. There was rarely any objection to including an item; the discussion usually led to clarifying the definition and also had the result of adding new ideas. We ended with a list of roughly 100 steps. We then turned afresh the next day to the electromechanical industries, went through the same exercise, and wound up with a practically identical list, except for differences in terminology.

A short time after the meeting I circulated the two lists to all the participants, but no one offered corrections, a good proof that we had done a creditable job in the first place. A revised list has been published a few times, with minor improvements and some additions, but I have yet to encounter any basic objections.

Exploratory Work Preparatory to a Development Project

The steps involved are: the conception of an idea for a new product or process; preliminary analysis to justify the belief that it lies within the objectives of the management; consideration of the probability of practical application; initial investigation of its parameters to define its potential; decision to propose an applied project to develop the idea further.

Development Stages

1. Product Definition. This stage involves the following steps: objective investigation of the utility of the concept; development of screening methodology to confirm practicality; initial estimate of commercial advantages; development of method for small scale preparations of materials; preparation and evaluation of a series of products for evaluation of utility by the screening procedures; selection of those individual products which show most promise; recommendation that further work be done to develop a refined method of preparation, coupled with initial study of commercial potential.

As the work progresses, preliminary answers should be sought for the following questions: performance requirements; availability and cost range of principal raw materials; market size and type; distribution system for this type of commodity; rough cost estimation, as for example, in some types of fine chemicals the selling price may be in the range of four times the yield-corrected raw material cost; critical examination of the competitive situation; preliminary consideration of patent situation; estimaton of probable minimum economic size of production unit.

The preparation of small samples for evaluation should involve the following precautions: selection of representative raw materials and special ingredients; examination of method of preparation from the point of view of manufacturing practicality; determination of stability and storage requirements; procedures for quality and process control; initial packaging concept; preliminary process flow diagram; selection of range of representative small samples for internal evaluation.

The steps involved in internal evaluations are: selection or development of testing methods; development of tests reflecting actual conditions of use; appraisal of performance of representative samples in comparison with competitive products; production cost review with manufacturing manager; market review with sales manager; initial consideration of special problems such as hazards in manufacturing, shipping, or use; types of customer specifications and information brochures, etc.

At the conclusion of this stage, if the prospects for the product remain favorable, the following conclusions should be justified: a product, which is believed to conform to management's plans for growth, has confirmed potential for marketability, insofar as this can be determined by internal appraisal, and can be made by a process which appears to be practical.

2. **Process Definition.** Small-scale work only has been done on the process, and the findings need to be examined more critically in large laboratory (or machine shop) or pre-pilot equipment. After this

Sequential Task Forces 53

work has been carried far enough to provide a prototype of commercial operations, the preparation of larger samples for submission to potential customers can be begun, because their comments on utility may require further adjustments in process which will need to be incorporated in semifinal design of operations.

The component steps include: study of the laboratory procedure in terms of feasibility of large scale production, equipment requirements, materials of construction, methodology for quality and process control; systematic investigation on intermediate scale of all these points to provide a perfected plan for production operations; preparation of a revised flow diagram; improved estimates of plant investment and operating costs; preparation of samples of product for field tests; modification of process to give a product which is believed to meet market requirements; review of process data to submit semi-final process description and estimates of production economics, including capital investment; initial draft of operating manual; evaluation of packaging concept.

This work, then, should reaffirm the conclusion that a perfected process will produce satisfactory commodities, as far as initial field tests can reveal, and that revised estimates of operating and plant costs are believed to be acceptable.

3. **Product Evaluation.** The findings of internal evaluation by laboratory methods and expert opinion may or may not be confirmed by the reactions of potential customers when they make actual trials of the products. The procedure by which this investigation is carried out is usually termed "market research". There are separate techniques for industrial products and consumer products, which will be summarized below.

In large companies these studies are carried out by staff groups which are variously called market research, market development, or corporate development departments; in planning the field testing programs they should seek the advice of the regular sales department. In small firms they are done on a part-time basis by a salesman, but he should be selected because of his alertness to the possibilities of new products, his objectivity in interpreting the reactions of potential purchasers, and his patience in conducting field tests.

For industrial products the procedure is carried out by submitting samples to selected customers for use in trial runs in their operations. The steps are: review of the results of internal evaluation; planning the details of the field test program, keeping the volume of samples as low as possible to reduce the expense of making them on small equipment; selecting the customers who will be invited to participate because of their attitudes toward adopting new products, and confirming the choices with the sales department; working with these customers in conducting the test runs; analyzing the results of customers' trials to determine needed changes in composition or form; arranging with the process developers to revise the process to meet the new requirements; continuing field testing to reach a conclusion as to market acceptability.

For consumer products the procedures of "consumer research" are used. In essence they consist of submitting samples to a "jury" of consumers to obtain their opinions of the merits of the products. The sequence of steps is the following: reviewing the findings of internal evaluation; planning a testing program, preferably by blind scoring with the inclusion of a technique for eliminating participants whose opinions appear to be without value, (such as a triangular test with two duplicates and a single sample to determine whether the respondent can detect the duplicates); discussing the requirements for samples with the process developer; preparing suitable packaging to ensure blind scoring; selecting a representative jury; conducting the tests; analyzing the scores; discussing modifications of the new product to secure higher acceptability; conducting further consumer tests to establish the fact that the product has promising market potential. To eliminate the possibility that first reactions of the jury may be unduly favorable because of the novelty of the test product, an additional procedure may be used to determine continuing satisfaction (satiety in the case of some products), by extending the tests over longer periods.

In evaluating both industrial and consumer products, the following additional steps are necessary: investigation of pricing, packaging, and promotional requirements; study of the structure of the market and competition to formulate a strategy and procedure for market entry; review of marketing costs, including direct sales and distribution expense, discounts and allowances for middlemen customary to the particular trade, and estimates of promotional expense.

At the end of this stage it should be possible to state that there

Sequential Task Forces

appears to be a marketing opportunity of sufficient volume and profitability for a product made by the preferred process in a plant of at least minimum economic size.

Confirmation Stages for Product, Process, and Cost-Benefit Analysis

The results of the work in Development Stages discussed in the preceding section should provide strong evidence of the probability of success in those projects which have passed the criteria of feasibility. This gives, in many cases of products similar to existing commodities, sufficient confidence in practicality to warrant direct commercialization, but even here a comprehensive review of all aspects is recommended before the final decision is reached. When the degree of novelty is high, however, there is need for further confirmation on what may be considered semi-commercial scale.

1. Confirmation of Process Feasibility. To make more certain the practicality of the process, the scale of investigation is stepped up to pilot plant or semi-works size. It is considered good engineeirng practice for operations that are innovative to limit the increase in size to not more than ten times that of the preceding throughput. If the project requires a very large plant, there may be four or more levels of scaleup, for example, laboratory, pre-pilot, pilot, semi-works, small commercial and finally full commercial.

The cost of installing and operating a pilot plant is very high. In the first place, the investment in a pilot facility and all adjuncts should be computed with the same care that would be used for a commercial plant. Secondly, pilot plant operation usually requires a comparatively large staff of engineers for supervision, and this may mean in continuous process at least one development engineer per shift for each major part of the process. Further, an isolated pilot facility requires auxiliaries corresponding to a commercial plant for receiving raw materials, storage, handling product, machine shop, etc.; it is therefore beneficial in many ways to locate plants of this size adjacent to a full size factory, with the added advantage that it can be used from time to time for other investigations. Finally, measurement of throughput is likely to be somewhat lacking in accuracy, unless great care is taken in calibration of the equipment. Personally, I prefer to rely on a well-instrumented pre-pilot unit for mass balances. On the other hand, for energy balances the larger scale is usually preferable.

For these reasons I recommend the following precautions regarding

the use of pilot plants:
1. Freeze specifications of product and definitions of process as far as possible before beginning operation.
2. Do not use a pilot plant for research except where definitely necessary because this scale is too expensive for investigative work; instead consider it a facility for confirming feasibility of doubtful steps in operations. (Make your mistakes on the smallest scale possible!!!)
3. Do not use a pilot plant as a commercial production unit except as required by urgent need to enter a market rapidly; it is below minimum economic size and the cost of professional supervision and change orders is high.
4. Consider the possibility of piloting only certain process steps, using other available equipment wherever feasible.
5. Do not pilot unless this scale is considered obligatory.
6. Use temporary adaptation of small commercial installations wherever possible.

In developing countries there is much pressure for the use of pilot plants as evidence of the practicality of the development work. As a result there are many expensive installations in technologic institutions which lie idle most of the time. This same condition exists in some institutions in industrialized countries where a wave of enthusiasm has resulted in elaborate acquisitions. For developing countries I recommend in general that pilot plants not be erected until there is real demand from some industrial entrepreneur and that it then be located adjacent to his works.

The successive steps in developing the program for process confirmation are the following: comprehensive review of available data on process technology and economics; comprehensive review of product specifications, internal evaluation, and field test results; preparation of plan for pilot work, including time and cost schedule for design, quality and process control program, installation, and operation; estimate of cost and schedule of samples for market tests; definition of process details; study of possibility of integration of investigation with present commercial operations; scale-up of pilot plant design, with special reference to materials of construction, flexibility, analysis of special techniques, program for testing products, coordination with central engineering department; program for training foremen and operators; study of problems of by-product and waste disposal; detailed design of pilot plant; installation of facilities; revised draft of operating manual.

The steps in pilot plant operation are: training of operating crew; analysis and reduction of process variables; coordination of operating plan with manufacturing department; re-evaluation of products, by-products, wastes, and costs; freezing of specifications for samples for market testing; preparation and packaging of test samples; revision of product specifications, if required by results of market testing, and preparation of improved samples; review of adequacy of quality and process control procedures; revision of operating manual, including process control, and preparation of quality control manual; preparation of comprehensive recommendations for design of commercial facility including site requirements, waste disposal, special facilities, and semi-final estimates of plant investment and operating cost.

At the end of this stage it is possible to make firm recommendations regarding product specifications, operating procedures, commercial plant design, with revised cost estimates.

2. Market Confirmation. The findings from the product evaluation stage represent only the opinions of potential customers, without any commitments to purchase. The final test of the merits of a product is willingness to buy it. Hence market potential is confirmed by offering the product for sale in a restricted market. The income received will not, in the vast majority of cases, cover the cost of manufacture on pilot scale.

In carrying out market testing on industrial products the following steps are usually taken: selection of a small number of customers to whom free samples are given for larger scale tests than were formerly used; analysis of results to meet any needs for revision of specifications; developing a final market test plan, including pricing, preliminary form of purchase contract (including escape clause if the project is not implemented on commercial scale), drafts of sales literature, etc.; sales campaign with a limited number of customers to minimize expense of pilot production; projecting potential market from this sample of purchasers.

For consumer products the following sequence is usually followed:

selection of a limited test marketing area or sample in cooperation with the sales department; planning details of the market development plan; preliminary promotional activities through publicity and give-away samples; offering the product for actual sale in a limited number of retail outlets; analysis of the results of test marketing to determine whether further changes in specifications or packaging are advisable; projecting the sales strategy and techniques when the project is commercialized; re-examination of sales expense estimates; projection of future sales volume.

At the conclusion of this stage, for a successful product, there is direct evidence of market demand for a commodity of the defined specifications, and projection of sales volume on commercial scale is believed to justify implementation.

3. Comprehensive Review Preparatory to Commercialization. This is a vital stage in development work. Failure to include it can cause severe penalties to the enterprise. In innovative projects, some of the earlier stages may have been carried out a few years before, and new technologic factors may have arisen since that time. Further, analysis of all facets of the undertaking should be conducted together.

This stage should be carried out with the management acting as coordinator. Representatives of all departments which have participated in the program should be required to reaffirm that the project is attractive. This includes up-to-date opinions regarding technology, raw materials, production, marketing, legal questions, and cost-benefit relationships. Only when this information is available does the management have adequate background for reaching a decision to commercialize the concept.

Implementation Stages

For completeness, a summary of the steps necessary for commercialization is given below. Even though this is somewhat outside the scope of the main subject, nevertheless there is justification for including it because many of the functional groups involved in earlier stages should participate.

1. Initial Steps for Commercialization: The steps required are: final review of market, sales costs, pricing, estimated profits, competition, distribution system, etc.; site selection for the plant, including marketing considerations, raw materials, utilities, transportation,

Sequential Task Forces

location-imposed restriction such as taxes and waste disposal problems, availability of labor and specialized staff, land availability and cost; detailed design of facilities to conform to the requirements of the selected site.

2. **Mobilization for Manufacturing.** The sequential steps are as follows: preparation of manufacturing plan and schedules; construction of facility; negotiation of firm contracts for raw materials and supplies; training of supervisors and operators; final draft of manuals for production, process control, and quality control; tune-in period to confirm satisfactory design and construction of plant, and suitability of product, process, and control procedures.

3. **Mobilization for Marketing.** Preparation of detailed sales program; preparation of sales and promotional material; sales training program; negotiation of sales agreements and contracts.

4. **ON STREAM.** Acceptance of operation for regular manufacture and sales, and setting up of normal schedule for quality and process control and for technical service.

Short-Cuts in the Use of the List of Development Steps

The complete list of stages and steps is aimed at innovative new products, for which there are many uncertainties both in regard to production problems and to their appeal to customers.

When the product resembles closely those already being made and sold by the company, there is much less room for doubt about its acceptability. When its composition and specifications have been defined sufficiently for the marketing department to estimate sales potential, production and marketing may be started on the basis of laboratory information only. This speeds up market entry and cuts the cost of the development effort. Even if the product does fail to live up to expectations and has to be quietly dropped from the line, no great loss has been incurred. It may be desirable to confirm the process on large laboratory or pre-pilot scale, but even that refinement will not involve much time or expense.

Many new ventures are started by smaller firms on the basis of known technology and know-how, which they have merely to adapt to their particular requirements. The information may be available from the trade literature or from vendors of equipment or raw materials. There may be government or state agencies, state university extension services, trade associations, or other sources of help. Sometimes larger companies are sources of assistance to their suppliers of components. The small firm can therefore place confidence in the reliability of the information because it has been used successfully by others.

The situation of the small firm in a developing country is much less satisfactory, because the complex of sources of help has not been so well developed. There are a few cases, notably Singapore and Argentina, where concerted efforts are being made to fill the gap. Even in industrialized countries the need for assistance to small enterprises is being increasingly recognized, and the programs in Canada, Japan, and the Netherlands are notable steps in this direction.

The subject of technology transfer is attracting much attention in many circles, but so far it is mostly discussion with little practical effect. The term is much too narrow, because it is not merely technology but also the whole business complex of skills which has to be transplanted. I much prefer the expression "transfer of commercial systems" as being more realistic. Mention is often made in discussions of technology transfer of the fact that cultural differences have to be taken into account in adapting knowhow from one country to meet the needs of another. Cultural differences play an even greater role in the practices of general management and marketing.

CHAPTER FIVE

MANAGERIAL CONTROL OF TASK FORCE SYSTEMS

Good management practices require a balancing of effort against the expected benefit to be obtained from different activities. A project system is a preferred technique for this purpose as a means of subdividing the total program into segments which can be defined, planned, carried out, and evaluated.

To establish a control procedure, the obvious thing to do is to account for distribution of time by the individuals involved in the work. This type of analysis measures the expenditure of effort in different activities. Of course, it does not purport to estimate the quality of this effort, which is a subjective appraisal to be made by other means.

Many organizations using project systems have adopted the device of time cards for reporting the number of units of effort spent by individuals on specified types of work. They have found through experience that without this precaution they can not determine how well the competence of staff has been used in meeting its objectives. Frequently the reporting is confined to major lines of work, on the assumption that the time not spent on these has been directed toward other useful activities.

The author contends, however, that effective management requires a complete breakdown of available time to include all types of activities. These include major projects, miscellaneous short-term assignments, and particularly non-project or overhead activities. These major categories will be discussed in this order in subsequent sections.

When time-accounting is introduced, it should be made clear that the system is being used for managerial purposes in allocating staff capabilities, and is not a disguised form of attendance record, which if needed can be obtained by other means such as a time-clock. Further, the mere statement that this is the purpose is not enough, but there must be continuing evidence that supervisors are employing the information in a managerial capacity, and are trying to assist the individual employee in making better use of his time.

Time-Accounting for Major Projects

In Chapter Three the methodology for setting up a task force has been described. This includes the preparation of a table of the amount of effort expected from the various team members. Some of these may be located in departments of the company which do not use time-accounting procedures, but, in negotiations for securing their services to participate in the work, it is often necessary to provide an estimate of the extent of their involvement. If this is done, there should be, as a protection against complaints of abuse of the privilege, a suitable record of the time they have actually spent.

The unit of effort to be measured may be a man-month, a man-week, a man-day, a man-hour, or other convenient measure. Experience shows that a man-hour is the best basis for most organizations, and it is therefore recommended. A man-day is likely to be broken up by other activities to such an extent that its significance is doubtful. The system the author is accustomed to in consulting work is the quarter-hour interval, which is a practical unit, but probably too short for general use. Some organizations use six minutes—one-tenth of an hour—for reporting, but this appears to be unnecessarily short and may involve so much trouble that it is honored by the breach rather than conformance. Whatever unit is selected, it should be adopted as a long-term procedure. Setting first a larger unit and then shortening it by steps will merely bring about arguments each time a reduction is made.

Assuming that the organization follows the author's advice and adopts one hour as the reporting unit, each member is required to submit a periodic report of how he has allocated his time to one or more major projects and to miscellaneous other activities. A weekly time card is most satisfactory to avoid excessive labor in compiling the totals, and the deadline for receiving the report should be rigorously enforced. Even in the case of individuals who are away from their posts, a supervisor or secretary can submit an estimate which can later be corrected if necessary.

The framework for reporting should be the total of available time without deductions for holidays or vacations which can be set up as separate account numbers. For an organization operating on a five-day week this will amount to 52 five-day weeks, and usual experience will be roughly 220 net working days exclusive of weekends (52 times

Managerial Controls 63

5 minus 20 working days vacation, minus 10 holidays, minus 10 days sick leave).

The typical work record of a senior technical man for six four-week periods might be that shown in Table 6. In this tabulation short-term technical assignments ("minor projects") and overhead activities, which will be discussed later, are shown for the sake of completeness.

The handling of overtime as a charge against projects is optional. In some cases it is reported as actually accumulated, which will give a total of net working time larger than the normal. In others, it is left up to the individual who may use it to increase the number of hours spent on project work with corresponding reduction of that on overhead activities.

It is common experience to have some members of the organization vocally resistant to the idea of reporting their time allocation. As time goes on they become used to the system and most of the complaints die out. The usual objections, and answers thereto, are the following:

"It is unprofessional"; but many individuals of high qualifications have been doing it for years, even when not required, as a means of budgeting their time.

"It is a sneaky way of checking attendance"; this is nonsense if the system is used for managerial purposes, as it should be, and not as a disciplinary device.

"It takes too much time from work to try to analyze everything I have been doing"; anyone who is not trying to be recalcitrant can do it in a very few minutes a day by entering into the spirit of the scheme and realizing that the figures are at best approximations.

"These figures don't mean anything, because only ideas count, and I get my best ones while I am shaving"; if we only had a good measure of productivity of effort, we would use it, but because we do not have one we have to employ the handiest scheme available.

The primary user of the data on time expenditure is the team leader, who should receive as promptly as possible a weekly summary of man-hours charged against his project by individual members. Coupled with his estimate of progress, if he wishes to express in bar

Table 6
WORK RECORD OF AN INDIVIDUAL
For convenience time is shown in days rather than in hours and a 28 day month is assumed

Classification	Actual expenditure of man-days						
	Jan.	Feb.	Mar.	Apr.	May	June	Total
Major Projects							
Team leadership							
Project 101	8	6	5	1	8	1	29
Project 102	-	-	3	1	6	7	17
Team participation							
Project 103	-	4	3	-	-	5	12
Project 104	2	2	1	-	-	-	5
Project 105	3	-	1	-	-	1	5
Project 106	-	1	3	-	-	1	5
Minor Projects (Collective)							
Technical service (201)	2	1	-	-	1	-	4
Quality control (202)	-	1	1	-	-	2	4
Subtotal, technical projects	15	15	17	2	15	17	81
Subtotal, percentage of total net working time	75	75	85	10	75	85	67.5 (average)
Overhead Activities							
Holidays, including week ends, and vacation	8	8	9	22	8	9	64
Illness	-	3	-	-	2	-	5
Professional meetings	3	-	1	1	-	2	7
Professional development	2	-	1	-	3	-	6
Unassigned	-	2	-	3	-	-	5
Subtotal, overhead	13	13	11	26	13	11	87
Total	28	28	28	28	28	28	168

Managerial Controls

chart form degree of completion of task, he can keep track of how well things are proceeding in terms of the approved project outline. He may need to find out what difficulties have caused one individual to spend so much time to achieve so little in the way of results. He may be concerned because another is not living up to his commitment and may therefore be threatening the schedule of others because necessary input of information will be delayed. If the difficulties are serious, he may need to have his estimate of effort or target date changed before the situation has deteriorated beyond retrieval.

Budgetary Control of Projects

Many organizations which use project systems as a basis for distribution of the time of the staff also employ financial control procedures to check the cost of this time against an approved budget. The conversion of units of effort into the equivalent monetary value is frequently done in the accounting department. The figures may be reported back to the project leaders or those charged with supervision of overhead activities, although this is not necessary because they can rely upon the time expenditure records as a managerial technique. Recommended practice, however, is to give them the financial data, because in this way the organization as a whole becomes more aware of the value of time and is more inclined to consider cost-benefit relationships in the way its manpower resources are deployed.

The bases for calculating the costs of time vary widely, and comparison of figures from different organizations cannot be made accurately unless they are adjusted to identical terms. The recommended practice is to compute total costs, including not only direct salaries, but all overheads such as fringe benefits, out-of-pocket expenses for supplies and services, administrative overheads, and a figure representing the cost of using the facilities. When charges to project accounts are made on the basis of the salaries of specialized personnel, and all other costs are lumped as overhead, the latter will often amount to well over 100 per cent of direct salaries. Some organizations confine their accounting to direct salary costs, although this gives a distorted picture of the true expense of the work, and practice ranges all the way from these minimum figures to those which are realistic because they include all overhead.

The methods for arriving at salary costs also show variation. In some cases the average of all personnel engaged in project work is used, while in others the actual salaries are employed, although in some organizations this is thought to be undesirable because it discloses individual salaries which are considered to be confidential between the person and the management. The most satisfactory system is to use figures representing a range of salaries within a certain classification, for example, junior, intermediate, and senior personnel. The composite overheads to be applied are usually added as a fixed percentage of direct salaries.

The procedures used for charging individual items of expense also show much variation. The extreme is to enter even minor items against individual project accounts, which in the author's opinion is not worth the additional accounting expense, paper work, and irritation to the staff. The best scheme is to accumulate these details, except for large special purchases, under suitable headings in the books of account, and to distribute them pro rata according to salary costs. Even where this system is followed, some items of out-of-pocket expenses, such as travel and the like, continue to be charged to project accounts.

As a guiding principle, project accounting is a managerial tool, and for that purpose should be kept as simple as possible, because the accuracy is only as great as the care with which the project personnel charge their time; this must be recognized as just an approximation. Additional details of charges do not serve a useful purpose unless they become excessive, as, for example, in abuse of toll telephone privileges, and in such cases they can be corrected by other means. There is a hazard that over-enthusiasm for keeping track of small items, which of course must be properly entered in the records of the accounting department, will waste more effort than they are worth and will harm morale.

Control of Minor Assignments by Consolidation

Many types of service activities are allowed to expand to an unwarranted extent because of the difficulty of finding practical means of evaluating large numbers of small assignments. A common example is found in research departments which carry out some quality control and technical assistance functions for operating plants. The requests

Managerial Controls 67

for help gradually increase, and more and more of the effort of the technical staff is diverted from the main objective of developing new and improved products and processes for expansion of business. This is only one instance of the way in which a corporate function may dissipate its capabilities by over-responding to pressures for immediate help from other parts of the company.

This is not to be understood as negating the actual need for these day-to-day services. The point at issue is adequate scrutiny of their justification. When the requests pass from one department to another, or in a large organization from one section of a department to another, there is a tendency to accept them rather than cause a dispute. Each is small in itself, rarely large enough to warrant making an issue of it.

A first step is to find out the real magnitude of each activity. This can be done by setting up a small number of collective "project accounts" with overseers to inspect them, to which the expenditure of man-hours can be charged, and this can then be converted into financial equivalents. The departments involved can then analyze the cost-benefit merits of each type of service. The example may be cited of determining when a company is financially justified in setting up a patent department to carry out the internal preparation of patent applications instead of using outside counsel for this purpose. (Some companies have concluded that 10-12 filed patent applications per year is the break-even point.)

Once the cost of the service has been determined, managerial study can select the optimum solution. The issue can be brought to a head by proposing an interdepartmental charge; for example, the cost of quality control and trouble-shooting on plant problems is logically a production expense and should be absorbed by the manufacturing department. Or, the handling of travel reservations by the traffic department may require so much clerical time that the costs should be charged back to those groups which request this assistance.

Often it will turn out that policing of requests for service has been inadequate, and until the rising cost dictates remedial action some managerial device must be found to control it. Or, the size to which the activity has grown may indicate that the department receiving the assistance should build up its internal competence to handle the load.

In any case it is clear that service functions should be carefully examined as to their magnitude and justification. In addition to compiling the costs under blanket project accounts, a brief running record of the effort expended on each item will give a summary for managerial attention to improve effectiveness.

Management of Non-Project Activities

The wastage of time on overhead activities not directly coupled with the normal functions of a department or group can be even more of a drain on staff capabilities than that lost through excessive service activities. Managerial attention is infrequently directed to this source of inefficiency. There is often not even thought about them, much less an attempt to bring them into order.

If a project system is to be effective, these overhead activities must be subjected to the same type of analysis of time distribution. For this purpose, several overhead accounts should be set up, the control of which is made the responsibility of some senior members of the staff. To obtain a realistic idea of their size, the total of work days or hours in a year should be used as a base. Certain accounts are more or less "fixed," such as vacations, week-ends, and holidays, but because they may not apply equally to all personnel they should be accounted for in the analysis. Others, such as illness, are irregular, but it is surprising how many organizations do not try to find out the magnitude of this source of lost time among the salaried staff, although it is customary to keep these records for "hourly" personnel, since their pay is based thereon. In some organizations in the United States experience shows an average loss through illness of 10 - 12 days per year. Recognition of the importance of these absences and also of the fact that the effectivess of employees actually on the job is impaired through poor health of others encourages preventive medical services.

The loss of time from these factors may be considered unavoidable, but there are numerous other activities which can be brought into line by managerial attention, and even with improvement of morale, because the conscientious employee is more contented when he is constructively occupied. In some organizations the number, attendance, and length of committee meetings are excessive, a topic that is discussed at more length below. Many organizations have quite liberal policies regarding professional development, such as educational

Managerial Controls

opportunities and provision for attending external meetings, but these privileges are sometimes carried to excess by some individuals, while others are overlooked in distributing the benefits.

The number of overhead accounts should be kept as small as is adequate for the purposes of analysis of major uses of time. Some employees will regard reporting of these categories as a chore, so that the irritation should be kept at a low level by explaining the managerial purposes of the scheme. Rather than to increase the number of accounts, it is better to make spot checks of those activities which are judged to warrant an inquiry in depth.

If the staff is to carry out reporting of time distribution, it is necessary that they have working definitions of the overhead accounts. Vacations, holidays, and illness are self-explanatory. Other classifications should be selected by the management to suit the convenience of the organization, but some examples that are listed below may be helpful. "Administration" is an account that needs to be included, but charges against it are usually limited to personnel at the managerial level, who include only the time spent in policy making, procedure development, and general administrative activities, the remainder of their effort being distributed over other overhead and project activities. "Personnel" also will be used mainly by individuals at higher echelons to record time spent in recruiting, indoctrinating, assessing performance, and handling individual administrative matters for the group reporting to them. "Internal contacts" may include meetings and conferences on policy matters, liaison with other parts of the organization on subjects not directly related to authorized projects, and discussions relating to concepts in process of formulation. "External contacts" cover entertainment of visitors, public relations, and the development of helpful liaison. "Professional development" includes courses given in other institutions or internal training sessions, attendance at professional meetings, general library reading, and time spent in preparing papers for publication.

Management of the reporting system for overhead activities should be flexible, and sympathetic. The main purpose is to determine whether the total effort being spent in these directions is suitable for the objectives of the organization. The break-down into different accounts assists individuals to separate out the time they spend on non-project activities and to make the management aware of the relative emphasis among them.

Systematic Deployment of Staff Efforts

The primary purposes of time distribution systems is to provide managers at all levels with data on which to analyze the way the staff is allocating its efforts in comparison with its mission, and to provide all individuals with an opportunity to improve their performance by studying their own work patterns. The latter function is a major step in the development of managerial capabilities throughout the organization. It throws increasing responsibility on the personnel to use their talents most effectively, thus relieving the managers of the detailed drudgery of administration and permitting them to participate directly in project activities.

The functions of a manager under this system are best illustrated by the example shown in Table 7. Here the head of a section is charged with the responsibiilty of seeing that his group is deployed to best advantage, either through their own efforts to obtain a suitable work level, or through the assistance he can give them.

The mechanism for compiling a tabulation of this type is quite simple if the staff is accustomed to working on a project system. In a group of this size, the section head can obtain a few days in advance by discussions with the members their estimate of work-load for the next four (monthly) periods. By experience he learns which ones are inclined to be over-optimistic and which ultra-conservative so that he can adjust the figures accordingly to obtain a realistic forecast. This is a basic managerial function. In larger groups he may call on some individual to assist him in gaining the information.

As a basis for determining adequacy of work load, some arbitrary norm for satisfactory performance should be selected. The experience of self-supporting consulting organizations provides some useful guidelines. Assuming a five-day week, which leaves 365—104=261 working days, an enterprise of this kind is likely to find that an average of roughly two-thirds of this available time of all staff members needs to be devoted to client projects at usual rates in order to maintain its overheads at competitive levels. When the number of working days is corrected for vacations (average 15 days), holidays (average 10 days), and absences for illness (average 11 days), only 225 days remain. If the necessary chargeability ratio ($2/3$ of 261=174) is to be

Table 7
ESTIMATE OF TIME DISTRIBUTION FOR A DISCIPLINARY GROUP

Individual	Classification	Estimate Time to Projects Allocation in Percent			
		Jan.	Feb.	Mar.	Apr.
Jones	Section Head	50	30	20	20
	Project Team Leaders				
Smith	Senior Staff	70	50	40	30
Smithfield	″ ″	60	60	80	50
Smithy	″ ″	50	80	60	20
	Project Team Members				
Wakefield	Junior Staff	80	80	80	70
Waldemar	″ ″	70	60	50	30
Walker	″ ″	40	90	60	20
Wall	″ ″	60	70	40	30
Winkelman	″ ″	50	66	60	20
Averages		53	58	49	31

attained, the client work must account for about 80 percent of this time, leaving an average of only one day per week for all overhead activities.

No comparable data are available from industrial organizations. In view of the fact that various service departments such as research and development, which provide specialized assistance to the rest of the company, are in the broad sense acting as consultants, it seems logical to propose that they might consider a similar standard for performance. Instead of providing assistance to clients on a fee basis, they are carrying out work on projects endorsed by top management and operating departments with approved budgets for amount of effort and cost. In some firms the central laboratory and other service groups actually have to sell their services to the rest of the organization, and their success or failure influences their staff size and rate of growth. Is it not a reasonable assumption, to ensure the proper orientation of their activities, that they should strive to devote 80 percent of their working efforts to authorized projects, including those covering collective minor assignments, and only 20 percent to overhead activities at their own selection?

Turning to the specific managerial problems illustrated in the chart, it is now the responsibility of the section head to see to it that the staff maintains a satisfactory work load. In this typical example of a service group, with a mixture of longer-range projects and short-term service assignments, it is usually difficult to project the work pattern more than a few months ahead. In a well-managed operation, however, this should give the administrative head sufficient lead time to assist his staff in obtaining new commitments to round out their programs. If they were in a self-supporting consulting group they would have to do this if the organization is to remain viable. This means that all members must find ways to sell their services to the rest of the company, a requirement that builds initiative and imagination.

Thus, in the example shown, the work load for the current period is below norm; for some reason or other, either lack of internal effort or adverse situations among their potential project sponsors, the desirable level of assignments has not been obtained. The next period appears to be satisfactory, because other new assignments, in addition to those already scheduled, are a reasonable expectation. Depending on past experience of the rate at which requests for work come in, the outlook for the third and fourth periods may be promising, doubtful, or disappointing. In no case should the section head relax his vigilance, because if he is so fortunate as to be faced with an excess of work, he can readjust assignments or can borrow personnel from some other group.

CHAPTER SIX

ENVIRONMENT AND BENEFITS OF INTERDISCIPLINARY TEAMS

From the preceding chapters it should be obvious that task forces of Type IV, and even Type III, require an environment that is radically different from the hierarchy of authority and responsibility shown in a typical organization chart. Such a structure does not provide the freedom of the individual to apply his abilities to problem solving, because it implies direct control by his immediate supervisor.

To achieve the proper interdisciplinary environment, two separate but complementary managerial systems must operate harmoniously in parallel: (1) the usual pyramidal structure to establish the framework within which the individual acts as a unit in the organization; and (2) the separate relationship which governs his participation in project teams under the guidance of individual project team leaders. They may be considered as the organizational and the activities systems, respectively.

The organizational system provides the policies and practices governing the place of the individual in the administrative structure. It defines the channels of general supervision of the way he conducts himself and applies his talents. It provides for appraisal of his performance and exerts managerial responsibility for rewarding his contributions. It serves as a resource for assisting with administrative problems which affect his project work.

The activities system, on the other hand, is the route through which he applies his skills to problem solving, as a member of groups of other specialists under the guidance of team leaders.

These two systems at first glance appear to be in direct conflict. That they can proceed smoothly side by side is proved by the experience of engineering groups over many decades. Gradually the scheme has been adopted for other types of activity. Those organizations which have used the principles would find a return to the formal structured pattern a source of frustration that would cause loss of morale and initiative.

The introduction of interdisciplinary teams into a cellular structure therefore requires basic alterations in managerial attitudes and behavior. An abrupt change from one style of operation to the other is likely to produce a temporary condition of chaos. Adoption of task force principles may be selective, however, to be used only for certain types of work. To assist those who would like to try out the system in an experimental way, the appendix, which is based on personal experience in initiating the procedures in numerous situations, is devoted to a discussion of the steps I have found useful for this purpose.

A basic requirement is adequate recognition of both professional performance and administrative ability. In a rigid cellular organization, the route to promotion is chiefly through managerial rank in the hierarchy. This has the disadvantage that talented specialists are often seduced into positions in which they become reluctant and mediocre administrators. Unless the value judgments are based on impartial appraisal of contributions to the success of the organization, problem solving abilities do not achieve their proper measure of reward.

Contrasting Patterns of Responsibility and Authority

In the time-honored structured organization, each level of management has direct control of both administrative functions and the actual work of the members in its chain of command. The managers schedule the activities, supervise them directly, appraise performance, and pass on their interpretations and recommendations to another echelon. In theory, coordination of inputs from different specialized areas is effected at those levels which are cross-over junctions. In practice, the need for better integration of competent opinions is often met by some form of review panel, or particularly by informal discussions among different specialists at the working level.

The pattern of flow of authority and information in formal organizations is too well known to require detailed discussion here. In general, the findings from the working level, developed according to the assignments given them, pass upward through supervisory layers until they reach a level thought to be suitable for transmission to other groups or departments in the organization. The comments of the recipients are reviewed and passed down again to the working level for consideration. The process is illustrated in the left side of Chart I on page 9.

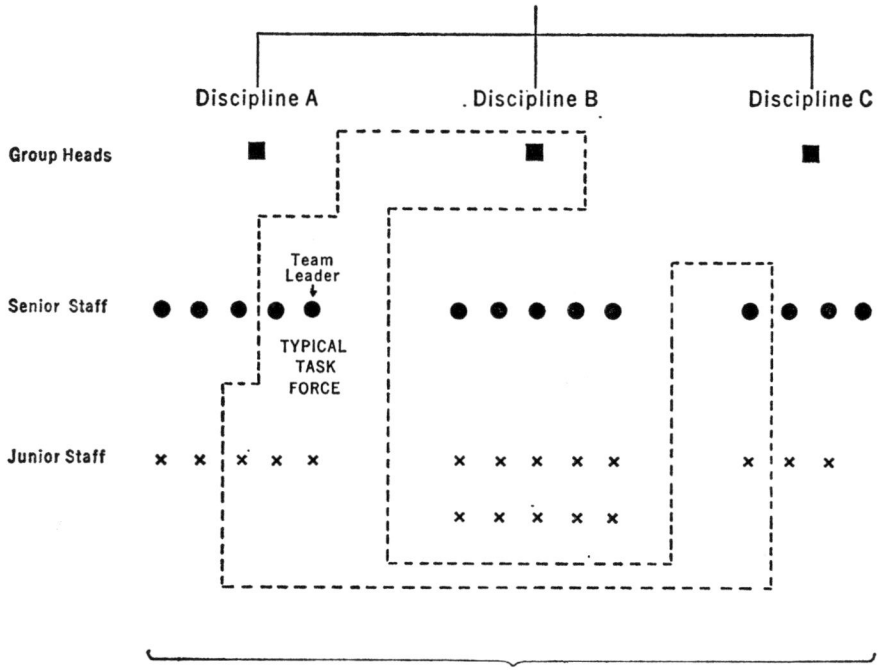

Environment And Benefits 77

The contrasting relationships in a system of interdisciplinary teams are shown in Chart IV. Disciplines A, B, and C are assumed to have different fields of specialization, such as, for example, applied research, engineering, and market research. Here there is a built-in mechanism for obtaining collaboration among different groups of specialists acting as a team to reach a common objective. The leadership of the team does not depend on administrative rank. Participation is often on a part-time basis. Position in the formal managerial hierarchy does not determine the seniority of the individual in project work.

Included in this diagram is the composition of a typical task force, indicated by the dotted area. The team leader is a senior staff member from Discipline A. He does not have direct administrative authority over any of the team members, but he is given delegated authority over that part of their activities devoted to the project for which he is responsible. Because the brunt of the work falls within the skills of Discipline A, the team includes an additional senior specialist and three juniors from this administrative unit; he does not have administrative jurisdiction over them, but only control over their project work. To complete the interdisciplinary mix, he has enlisted the collaboration of the head of Discipline B and one senior and one junior specialist from Discipline C.

The respective titles of Group Head and Senior Staff Member do not have any significance for their roles as members of the team. Junior Staff Members, however, are considered to be still in process of developing their skills, and would not be considered ripe for team leadership. In the diagram they have the function of working with a senior associate, usually to carry out some of the detailed work necessary for the contribution from that particular section. On the other hand, if in spite of his lack of professional maturity he had developed some form of specialized expertise, he might be assigned to contribute this function without the need for a more senior supervisor, provided the team leader decides that this representation is adequate for the success of the project.

Finally, the presentation of the findings to the user of the information, including the preparation of reports, is the responsibility of the team leader, acting on behalf of and with the cooperation of the other members. This is a notable departure from the procedure in a structured organization in which this function would be carried out by some one at a higher administrative level. This provision in interdisciplinary systems adds greatly to the morale and professional satisfaction of those at the working level. In many organizations which use task force systems, very senior and experienced individuals often prefer to devote themselves to project work instead of assuming duties of an administrative nature. Further, even the senior administrators themselves take some part in project activities, thus permitting them to contribute their professional competence and to keep aware of the problems of those exclusively at the working level.

Interdisciplinary Teams and Management Theory

The advantages of interdisciplinary teams for problem solving can be attributed to the fact that they exemplify the basic principles of all modern schools of management analysis. Koontz and O'Donnell have provided a valuable concept for coordinating these theories **(Principles of Management,** 1968, pp. 34-42). They consider that the dominant doctrine is that of the operational school because "it attempts to analyze management in terms of what managers actually do." They regard the five other principal schools—empirical, human behavior, social system, decision theory, and mathematical—as specialized aspects of operational management theory.

In pointing out how interdisciplinary teams fulfill the teachings of these six doctrines, the definitions of Koontz and O'Donnell will be used. The reader who wishes to go more deeply into the subject should turn to their excellent book which is also a cornucopia of citations to the original literature.

The operational school, regarded by them and also by this author as the unifying concept, "analyzes the management process, establishes a conceptual framework for it, identifies its principles, and builds a theory of management from them."

The empirical school "analyzes management by a study of experience, sometimes with interest to draw generalizations, but usually merely as a means of transferring experience."

The human behavior school "is based on the thesis that, since management involves getting things done with and through people, its study should be centered on interpersonal relations."

The social system school "is closely related to the human behavior school. . . . It includes those who look upon management as a social system."

Environment And Benefits

The decision theory school "concentrates on rational decision—the selection, from among possible alternatives, of a course of action."

The mathematical school "includes those theorists who see management as a system of mathematical models and processes."

Conformance with Operational Theory. An interdisciplinary team exemplifies the analysis of functional requirements and the logical programming of inputs and outputs of diverse specialized skills to achieve an objective. To make sure that all essential disciplines are included, the team leader must carry out some form of network analysis, either formal or informal, to determine the proposed level and timing of inputs from the array of specialists. When the assignment is one phase of a project involving a succession of major stages, undertaken by successive teams, the wise team leader will provide feed-back and feed-forward to insure continuity in development and application; this he can do by including key personnel from preceding functions and from those destined to become active later.

For large and complex projects, such as those in major defense or space programs, some type of Critical Path Method or Program Evaluation and Review Technique is required. For the more usual sort of R & D assignments or feasibility studies in industry, such elaborate procedures are not necessary, although the basic principles are used less formally by the skilled team leader. To promote efficiency in decision making, when the team consists of more than five or six members, it is advisable to select a small key team representing the dominant skills, and to use the others in a consulting capacity. This device avoids the inherent waste of time in large meetings when many of the participants are concerned with only parts of the subject matter, but the leader must make sure that each individual is kept informed of all pertinent activities on a need-to-know basis.

Empirical Expertise Is Effectively Utilized. When a team leader selects colleagues for a project, he puts a premium on expert knowledge and experience. Because the group is interdisciplinary, however, too much reliance on traditional know-how is counterbalanced by other members who will challenge stereotyped opinions. The pragmatic experience of experts from different disciplines is an essential ingredient to avoid impractical conclusions.

Individual Talents Are Put to Optimum Use. From the point of view of the human behavior school, it is hard to conceive of a procedure which provides a greater challenge to the individual to exert his abilities, with limitation only on the approach agreed to with the team leader for contribution to the common goal. He has joined the group as a volunteer in association with peers. He employs his creativity within his discipline to develop the details of his own attack, and he is free to express his opinion on the programs of the other members of the team.

Group Dynamics is an Essential Feature. The ideal team strives to perform as a unit. The give-and-take of informal team discussions leads to constructive criticism of individual ideas. The members are encouraged to test their concepts openly within the jury of the brotherhood. If the ideas are sound, but require adjustment for application to the problem, open discussion will lead to their modification to useful dimensions. Incidentally, differences of opinions among team members may at times be very deep-seated; reconciliation of diverging views requires a high order of ability on the part of the team leader to maintain a healthy climate in the group.

Decision Theory is Inherent in Team Procedures. The nature of the group activity leads to systematic testing of concepts and conclusions against alternatives. This provides a continuum of decision making, with close-coupled feed-back in broad perspective because of representation of varied disciplines. As an example, activities of successive teams carrying a new product concept to commercialization may need to make feasibility decisions at 100 or more distinct steps.

Mathematical Analysis is Often a Valuable Tool. In a well-rounded organization, many teams include members or are headed by specialists in operations research methodology. These are free to seek out and to apply mathematical analysis and model building wherever they can be shown to be useful. At the very least, they contribute to the systematic planning of investigations and to evaluation of the limits of accuracy in the conclusions.

Development of Managerial Capabilities. In addition to embracing the principles of the various theories of management, interdisciplinary teams provide the participants with on-the-job training in managerial practices. They afford concrete experience regarding those techniques which are effective in project leadership. The internal pressures on each individual to attain optimum contribution toward the goal lead

Environment And Benefits 81

him to better programming of his work to maintain planned performance.

Benefits of Interdisciplinary Systems

The scope of the foregoing material justifies a summary of the benefits which should result from the adoption of the principles of interdisciplinology. These are divided in this section into two parts: (1) those accruing to the organization and (2) those relating to the opportunities for the development of the individual. From my point of view, there are no real disadvantages except for the necessity for managers to conduct a thoroughgoing review of their policies and practices, which I consider to be an incentive to better administration and not a deterrent.

The examples given in earlier chapters will surely appear to some readers as too sophisticated for widespread use. I admit that the procedures described will not be carried out with entire success according to the models until the organization has gained enough experience to understand thoroughly the principles and their implications. This requires modifications in policies, practices, and administrative relationships. From personal experience in installing the system in a variety of groups, I have found that the changes are not hard to make provided the key managers approach the ideas in a constructive way rather than disputing their validity. The concepts are, in general, welcomed at the working level because they provide the individuals an opportunity to participate in projects in a way that gives them greater satisfaction in their roles. If appropriate activities are selected for a trial period, in the course of a few weeks or months performance reaches a satisfactory level and directions for improvement become evident. Then the system can be expanded to other activities which are judged to be susceptible to this approach.

Even when an organization adopts the procedures only in part, or merely on a token basis, the effect is often beneficial. The reconsideration of managerial principles, particularly the greater recognition to be accorded to the views of those at the working level, tends to stimulate a groundswell toward more open structures and communications.

Benefits to the Organization. The listing below gives my views of the advantages obtained by the use of interdisciplinary teams:

Greater effectiveness in the use of human resources through more critical control of expenditure of effort, which leads to better appreciation of the real value of expertise;

Stimulation of a sense of purpose throughout the staff as a result of more incisive selection, appraisal, and planning of programs through the direct involvement of all participants;

Speeding up of problem solving by effective and timely feed-in of information and opinion from competent sources;

Acceleration of implementation as a result of forewarning to new levels of participation by means of their earlier involvement in the collaborative endeavor;

Prompter recognition of major obstacles to feasibility in time to change direction of program or to curtail activity;

Continuity in the transfer of knowledge and expertise from one group to another;

Reduction of "empire-building" in groups by providing a smooth channel for using skills available elsewhere in the organization;

Elimination of redundant levels of supervision with resultant shorter lines of communication in a flatter organization;

Development among the staff of more versatile competence and improved managerial skills through interaction with co-workers on a wider range of problems;

Improvement in information retrieval through a network of specialists, each having familiarity with his own area of expertise;

Better personnel evaluation through a wider range of opinions from co-workers.

Benefits to the Individual. A well organized task force system places greater responsibilities upon the teams and their members and, at the same time, gives them more freedom in applying their skills. In smoothly running organizations, the team leader designs the work outline, subject to managerial approval, selects specialists to supply the required expertise, and invites them to serve in the group, usually on a part-time schedule, in the capacities which he has planned. He recognizes their competence, without being an expert himself in some of the disciplines represented, and is familiar enough with the nature and the techniques of these specialized areas in relation to the ob-

Environment And Benefits

jective, so that he is able to inject their contributions effectively into the total effort. This really means that each team member is essentially a volunteer.

This participative role enhances each team member's sense of professional opportunity because of the following incentives:

Increased confidence in and loyalty to the organization as a whole;

Personal responsibility for planning and carrying out special functions which he has participated in defining;

Improved managerial ability for the use of his own expertise to accommodate it to the total program;

Greater sense of achievement through better knowledge about the advances of projects on which he has worked toward commercialization;

Increase in professional self-confidence through maintenance of status in a composite group of peers;

Increased skill in interpersonal relations through the experience of close cooperation with other team members;

Enrichment of understanding of other areas of specialization;

Enhancement of ability to communicate with representatives of other disciplines and functional groups;

Opportunity to evaluate his innovative ideas with a peer group before submitting them to the more conservative managerial hierarchy.

CHAPTER SEVEN
TASK FORCES FOR CORPORATE DEVELOPMENT

Every well-managed organization should establish a mechanism for planning its future. Unless this activity is recognized as a separate specific function, it will not receive the orderly attention which it deserves. Also, the techniques for analytical consideration of alternatives will rarely be adopted.

Many large companies have set up interdisciplinary staff groups to perform this function. They are often called corporate planning or corporate development groups. They generally report to the chief executive or to another high official. They serve in an advisory capacity and in many firms their members devote full time to the activity, supplementing their personnel resources by borrowing from other units.

The skills of these groups normally include the techniques of planning, industrial economics, and cost-benefit analysis. They often have other technoeconomic capabilities such as marketing research. They should be kept small in size so as not to duplicate unnecessarily the skills available elsewhere in the organization. They should carry out many of their studies by task forces incorporating personnel borrowed from other departments; this procedure provides better knowledge of practical considerations, a welcome form of professional development for these associates, and a means of spreading the use of planning concepts and methodology more widely in the organization.

The first step in organized planning should be an objective assessment of company resources—both strengths and weaknesses—but unfortunately this is often pushed aside by pressure to undertake more immediate projects. High priority should be given to the initial formulation of a corporate development policy, a systematic development plan, and criteria for the evaluation of specific proposals. Sometimes a product policy is also established to give more specific guidance to those concerned with expansion of the product line. These activities will be discussed in detail in later sections.

A Systematic Program for Corporate Development

The rest of this chapter is devoted to a summary of the methodology which my associates and I have used with success in many studies carried out for clients. The procedures have proved to be so helpful that frequently they have been adopted for internal use on a continuing basis by these firms or agencies.

The basic principle is to subject a comprehensive list of potential opportunities to analysis from two points of view: (1) the characteristics these micro-sectors of industry have shown in the general economy, and (2) the extent to which corporate resources are adequate for undertaking them.

To provide background for this analysis, an objective assessment of internal skills and other resources should first be carried out. Then criteria should be selected and defined as a basis for the step-wise evaluation of the opportunities. At the same time, policies and programs for development activities can be formulated to aid the appraisal.

All these procedures should be undertaken with the understanding that their period of validity is flexible. Changes can take place both in internal resources and in the external economy. Hence the findings and the premises on which they are based should be carefully reviewed periodically—preferably at least once a year—to bring them up-to-date with the new conditions.

The order of discussion which will be followed is:

I. Assessment of internal resources;
II. Formulation of policies and programs;
III. Systematic appraisal of opportunities in seven successive steps, including the definition of criteria for evaluation. These steps are:
   1. Compilation of a checklist of industrial micro-sectors for consideration;
   2. Definition of criteria for evaluation;
   3. Scoring the general characteristics of the list of micro-sectors;
   4. Scoring this same list independently in regard to internal capabilities;
   5. Preliminary screening to select most promising candidates;
   6. Examination in depth of selected list of opportunities;
   7. Managerial decisions on courses of action.

Corporate Development

This appears to be a lengthy program, but initial use of its principles should not be delayed until the steps have all been carried out in sequence. The procedures should be based on their practicality for evaluation of individual opportunities. Most companies have already prepared some sort of listing of new ventures they wish to consider. By using these as test cases, the corporate development group is in better position to formulate policies, programs, and criteria. The entire process requires a gradual, continuous evolution, and, as criteria are sharpened, these revised methods of evaluation can be used to check earlier conclusions. An advantage in using consultants for installing the system is that they may already have available extensive lists of opportunities and definitions of criteria which can be adapted to fit the requirements of the organization.

Assessment of Internal Resources

Realistic growth plans must be based on an objective appraisal of the strengths and weaknesses of the company. Naturally, managers of individual functions can rarely be expected to take an unbiased view of the quality of their own activities. A corporate development department can organize such surveys on a more impartial basis. Smaller companies can set up special groups to carry out the task. Firms often use consultants to secure a still greater degree of objectivity for these assessments. And these evaluations should be updated as frequently as circumstances warrant.

Corporate capabilities can be grouped under six major headings: management, marketing, technology, raw materials, manufacturing, finance. The bearing of each of these on planning for growth is implied in the following outline:

Management: competence, depth, versatility, aggressiveness, structure; executive development programs; managerial policies which affect growth potential;

Marketing: nature and scope of franchise; structure, posture, competitive position, and versatility of sales staff for intensifying or diversifying the business; characterisitics of present distribution patterns and channels;

Technology: strength, versatility, and areas of expertise of the technical staff; relationships with management and operating departments; ability to promote and assist in commercializing new technology; extent of patent franchise;

Raw Materials: competitive position and alternate sources; coverage of direct control or purchase agreements for major raw materials, intermediates, and other supplies; facilities for receiving and storage; transportation costs;

Manufacturing: competence and special skills of the production organization; condition, flexibility, and location of plants;

Finances: internal resources; competitive position for raising additional capital.

Formulation of Plans for Growth

Progressive managements are turning more and more to the preparation of written plans for defining their governing policies for successful continuation and expansion of their businesses. Inherent in such planning activities is the necessity that they should be kept up-to-date, i.e., that they should be reviewed periodically. If they are not reappraised, they may get out of phase either with developments within the organization or with the competitive climate of the external economy. A decision for a major new commitment of the company will often dictate important revision of some aspects of the plans.

Development Policy. The general form that such a written policy for growth may take is indicated by the following typical questions. What should be the goal for increases over a period of years in rate of profitability and turnover? What are the expectations for these increases—or decreases—in different sectors of the business? Is there a preference among lateral diversification, forward integration toward new markets, integration backward toward starting materials, or a hold-your-own policy? What criteria should be used for evaluating ideas for new products? Does the management prefer to develop most of them internally, will it rely on acquisition to speed up growth, or will it follow a middle course? What funds, on what time scale, and with what expectation for return on investment will be available to finance expansion? What should be the relative emphasis on increasing the present business, and what on diversification into other markets? Should joint ventures be considered, or does the management hold to a go-it-alone policy? What preferences are there for types of markets to be considered for entry, and are there restrictions on others because they are felt to be incompatible with best use of the company's resources? Does the management wish to rely chiefly

Corporate Development 89

on internal generation of new technology, or is it inclined to negotiate licenses to acquire know-how and patent rights?

After acceptance of the proposed policy by management, copies should be distributed in the organization on a need-to-know basis. It provides general guidelines for those who are concerned with formulation and investigation of concepts for growth and diversification. In some cases it may summarize the status of projects already in process or scheduled for future work (i.e., a development program), but in others its purpose is to provide only a statement of policy.

Policies should always be sufficiently flexible to permit consideration of particularly attractive ideas that appear to be in conflict. If these are accepted, the policy statements should be revised in light of the new considerations which have arisen.

Development Program. Many companies believe it desirable to prepare a separate statement of activities already authorized or contemplated to provide perspective for considering new activities. This is particularly true in large firms with separate divisons whose fields may tend to overlap. Some of these documents are quite lengthy, giving not only descriptions of the projects but also the policy reasons for undertaking them. To provide for easy revision they may be issued in loose-leaf form. The separate statements of policy and program provide a basis for checking practice against theory, a comparison which should be helpful to each.

Product Policies. Growth policies and programs set the general framework of expansion planned by the management. More specific guidance is often desirable to provide criteria by which ideas for new products may be judged. A written product policy is found to be a valuable mechanism for this purpose. Like the corporate development plan for growth, it too should be dynamic and should be reviewed periodically.

Managers often fail to study in depth the impact on the business of different classes of additions to the product complex. It is quite usual to list or count the number of new products without discrimination as to the effect they may have on the market posture of the company. To provide a tool for this type of examination, I proposed in 1964 the breakdown (outlined below) into new items closely related to the existing product line, innovative new products, and new product lines. Their respective benefits and risks are shown in tabular form in Table 8. This scheme is being used by a number of companies for reviewing their product policies and for adjusting the thrust of their research and development programs.

A company applying this concept should primarily relate it to its own affairs, rather than to consider it with respect to the pattern of the sectors of industry in which it is engaged. Even though competitors may have pioneered in certain directions, the benefit and risks are individual to the firm, although both benefits and risks are reduced as a result of the prior entry of others. Thus a certain product may be counted on to succeed with more assurance because the experience of some other company provides evidence, but at the same time the rewards are likely to be less because of the existence of this competition. The new entrant must himself develop the necessary technology, marketing skills, manufacturing facilities and competence, and financial support. To him it is a new venture in spite of any evidence of the experience of someone else.

> **New Items** are products closely related to those already being sold by the company. They can be marketed with only minor modification of tactics, channels, or types of technical service required by customers.
>
> **Innovative New Products** enable the firm to satisfy customers' needs in a novel manner, but they are sold in the market areas already being served. They require special marketing effort and intensified technical service to bring about commercial acceptance.
>
> **New Product Lines** are new types of business. They lead the company into new areas of marketing. They require different sales strategies and channels of distribution.

Decisions on product policy must be based not only on management's aspirations for the company, but also on realistic weighing of resources versus new requirements for technology, marketing capability, production facilities and skills, and capital in the course they would like to follow. Participation in a task force approach to product policy formulation by key individuals from these areas of specialization, in addition to assisting in comprehensive evaluation of the prospects, also makes for keener awareness of the major objectives of the organization.

If the management decides that it wishes to exploit its present

Table 8
COMPARATIVE BENEFITS AND RISKS OF NEW ITEMS, INNOVATIVE NEW PRODUCTS, AND NEW PRODUCT LINES

Characteristics	New Items	Innovative New Products	New Product Lines
Relationship to Present Products	Closely related	Innovative	Usually very different
Managerial Aspects			
Profitability	Customary	Improved	Attractive
Impact on business	Re-enforced position	Increased penetration	Diversification
Risk	Routine	Considerable	High
Investment	Customary	Important	Large
Cost of market entry	Moderate	Increased	High
Period of development	Short	Longer	Very long, decreased by acquisition
Marketing Aspects			
Market analysis	Routine	Important	Demanding
Marketing channels	Same	Same	New
Marketing techniques	Same	More complicated More specialized	New
Marketing staff	Same	Continued from present business	New
Franchise (customer acceptance)	Same	Favorable	Must be established
Effect on present customers	Passive		Must be considered
Technical Aspects			
Technology availability	Easy	Must be developed	Harder to acquire
Development cost	Routine	Increased	High
Development time	Short	Longer	May be very long
Technical service	Customary	Considerable increase	New
Production Aspects			
Raw materials	Usually related	May be different	Usually different
Facilities	Customary	May be new	Usually different
Processes	Customary	May be different	Usually different

position by concentrating on expansion of its existing business, it will adopt a conservative stance toward new technology; research and development activities, the forerunner of innovation, will concentrate on product and process improvement and on new items related to the present line. There is nothing wrong with such a decision, because many companies do have unfulfilled opportunities in their own backyards. They may not have used to the full extent their resources of technology and operational capabilities.

The management may adopt, at the other extreme, a very aggressive attitude. They may decide that their business is locked into a sector of industry which is too restrictive in outlook for profitability and volume. They wish to break out of these restraints. A premium is to be placed on innovation. Research and development are to include a large share of work aimed at radically new products or on exploration of new technologies which may lead to new directions of expansion. Nevertheless, a substantial part of the technical budget, usually more than half, must still be directed toward defending the present market position.

Appraisal of Growth Opportunities

Corporate managements are faced continually with the difficult problem of choosing the best directions for growth to attain their planned objectives for the future. In many cases this selection is made in an informal way by the top executives on the basis of their judgment of an unweighted list of alternative opportunities. Intuitive hunches are likely to play an important part in their decisions.

The question is of great significance in planning the product development program. In many cases a period of five years or even more will elapse between the beginning of a long range investigation and implementation of the results on a commercial scale. It is true that the cost of R & D represents only 5 to 10 percent of the investment represented in full scale operation, but the number of successful projects out of the total program is bound to be quite low, because of obstacles encountered during the course of development. The pleas of research directors for better guidance from management on preferred directions of growth therefore have special relevance.

Over the years methodology has been developed in some organizations for systematic screening and evaluation of a gamut of subjects of potential interest. The procedures, which will be described in de-

Corporate Development

tail below, consist of the seven steps mentioned previously: (1) preparing a check list of industrial micro-sectors to be considered; (2) establishing criteria for evaluation; (3) assessing the general characteristics of each sector in terms of attractiveness; (4) making a separate appraisal of the entire list in comparison with the resources of the organization; (5) carrying out a preliminary screening to select those sectors that have both suitable potential and at the same time good fit to the company's capabilities; (6) conducting a more critical assessment of the candidates by examination in greater depth; and (7) deciding on the appropriate course of action for each micro-sector in the final selection.

The methodology requires inputs from economic, marketing, and technologic specialists, as well as from top management. The desirability of a task force is obvious. In companies which have established a corporate planning function, this group is often assigned responsibility for organizing the activity, making use as needed of skills from elsewhere in the organization.

The procedures will be outlined as seven sequential steps in the following sections. In Table 9 a convenient form of tabulation for the preliminary screening is given, based on the results of steps (1) through (4).

The methodology described is particularly suitable for large companies in highly developed economies. It can also be applied to diversification studies for smaller enterprises by simplifying the list of candidate opportunities, but the same types of criteria should be retained.

Compilation of List of Micro-sectors (Step 1). A comprehensive array of micro-sectors should be prepared in those broad types of industry which the management wishes to consider. The items should insofar as possible follow the sub-divisions under which published statistics are available, such as a census of manufactures, a tabulation of exports or imports, or the like. The more detailed the list, the greater the economic and technologic homogeneity in each sector, and therefore the more meaningful the findings of the analysis. For example, in scrutinizing diversification opportunities in fine chemicals, we have used arrays of several hundred raw materials, intermediates, and finished products.

As a specific example, let us consider the sub-classification of the food industry. In the statistics available in many industrial countries, there is first a break-down into major categories such as bakery products, canned fruits and vegetables, dairy products, frozen foods, and so on. Each of these is subdivided still further, e.g., under bakery products will be found biscuits and crackers, bread, cake and other sweet goods, etc. Much finer classification is desirable if enough information and data are available to provide a framework for appraisal.

Considerable care should be used in developing this list of industry sectors because it will form the matrix of classification for the future. The categories under which government statistics are collected are seldom rearranged because such changes would be disruptive of existing series of economic comparisons. New items may be added as a result of innovative expansion or present classifications may be subdivided as a consequence of growth in volume of the components, but these are usually the limits of alteration.

An array of sectors based only on a census of manufactures will necessarily omit novel products which are not being made in the country. These are especially interesting to companies oriented toward innovation. The gaps in the list may be filled from three sources, with increasing degrees of uncertainty: (1) articles imported from foreign countries; (2) products being made and sold abroad, but not yet in import; and (3) innovative commodities not in commerce anywhere.

Ideas for promising new sectors may be gleaned from statistics on imports. In these cases the prospective sales volume and price level will have been established. If the opportunity looks attractive, the company has only to determine whether it can generate or license the necessary technology and production skills.

Sometimes products being made and sold in foreign countries but never introduced on the local market look attractive. Feasibility depends on interpretation of sales acceptance abroad in terms of prospective customer appeal at home. Technology and manufacturing know-how must be acquired or generated.

Articles of completely innovative character which have never been marketed may come from a company's internal research program or from purchased rights to the inventions of others. Market potential must be estimated. A thorough investigation of customer acceptance on a pilot basis is necessary before launching a commercial venture. When the list of industrial sectors to be considered includes products

Table 9
SCREENING OF NEW PRODUCT OPPORTUNITIES
(Scoring System: H—High; M—Medium; L—Low)

Part A Evaluation of Industry Characteristics				Part B Array of Industry Sectors	Part C Fit to Corporate Resources			
Rate of Growth	Profitability	Ease of Commercial Entry	State of Technology		Marketing	Technology	Manufacturing	Investment
				Orderly listing of industrial sectors and their component micro-sectors in convenient form for analyzing completeness of coverage of possible opportunities				

for which there is no local history of production and sales, the potential benefits and risks must be very carefully weighed.

Definition of Criteria (Step 2). Attention should then be turned to formulation of the technoeconomic criteria by which each industrial sector will be characterized. Those that are adequate for most purposes are rate of growth, profitability, ease of commercial entry, and state of technology; they will be treated in more detail in following sections. To carry out the evaluations, a simple scoring system of high, medium, and low is satisfactory. For rate of growth and profitability, the dimensions of the scoring may be quantified, e.g., an average growth of 10 percent or more per year over a 5 or 10 year period may be rated as high, 5 to 10 percent as medium, and 5 percent or less as low. The other criteria are subjective in nature, but some definition should be prepared so that the ratings will be consistent. Other criteria which may be used are return on investment, restrictive regulations, and competitive situation.

Potential sources of information for applying these criteria are mentioned also in the next section. As time goes by, the data should undergo continual sharpening. The list becomes a valuable asset in formulating plans for growth and expansion.

In regard to criteria for use in Part C of Table 9, "Degree of Fit to Corporate Capabilities," four headings suffice for initial screening, viz, Marketing, Technology, Manufacturing, and Investment. It is difficult to apply them realistically unless the organization has first subjected itself to a comprehensive evaluation of its resources of the scope described on pages 87-88. The same system of scoring as high, medium, or low is used here also. The ratings are largely subjective, but it is helpful to have some form of definition of the three grades as a basis for reaching an opinion.

Scoring the Characteristics of Individual Micro-Sectors (Step 3). The criteria for this evaluation are applied successively to each item on the list and the scores of high, medium or low are entered in Part A of Table 9. It is well to provide a convenient method of making changes in the master record, because some of the ratings will need alteration in course of time as a result of variations in the national economic climate.

Suggested sources of information regarding the criteria are given in tabular form as follows:

Rate of growth: national industrial statistics; trade association publications and executives; financial periodicals and items in the daily or technical press; commercial and investment banks; confidential discussions with informed members of the industrial or financial communities.

Profitability: either as a percentage of turnover or return on investments: the same sources.

Ease of commercial entry: opinion as to probable success of a new venture, based on market analysis which takes into account the competitive structure of the industry, such as being dominated by a few large companies or made up of numerous small enterprises with limited local franchises. The internal investigation should be supplemented by informal discussions with bankers, trade association executives, and other well-informed individuals (note the later cautionary remarks about probable share of market).

State of technology: estimate by engineers and technologists of the state of the art, such as an advanced technologic background requiring extensive research and specialized know-how, or, at the other extreme, long-established manufacturing methods with a slow rate of innovation; the degree of domination by existing patent coverage needs to be taken into account.

Comparison of Opportunities with Organizational Capabilities (Step 4). The characteristics of a sector may look very attractive, as revealed in Step 3, but it may be entirely unsuitable when regarded from the point of view of the resources of the company. For example, it may require a very large capital investment for a plant of minimum economic size, as in the case of primary petrochemicals. Or it may involve advanced and rapidly changing technology, as in the production of electronic components. The marketing requirements may be very demanding, as they are in the pharmaceutical industry.

Those who have been involved in the development of a new product are likely to be enthusiasts who predict that it will sweep rapidly into command of a large share of the market. The facts of life are that this is unlikely in the face of strongly entrenched competition unless the product represents a high degree of innovation at little extra cost in its utility to customers. The competitors may be willing to accept a new entrant up to, say, perhaps 10 percent of the current market volume, especially if demand is growing. But if the newcomer seeks to enlarge his share by pricing policy, they are in better position than he is to defend their franchises, because their plant investments are partially or wholly written off and they have already absorbed the expense of developing the market. Sometimes there is a favorable factor in countries which endeavor to control monopolies in that a company which dominates an industry may be willing to assist a new entrant in order to induce a competitive climate.

The interdisciplinary evaluation group needs, therefore, to assess all the candidate sectors in the list, regardless of their rating for industry characteristics, in terms of the available resources of the organization. This set of scores should be recorded in Part C of Table 9. In reaching decisions, the task force should disregard Part A because it might introduce bias in the new appraisals. Both are included in the chart for convenience and to illustrate the entire process of selection of preferred sectors. In carrying out Step 4, it is hence advisable to cover up Part A by temporary masking.

The four criteria in the following tabulation have been found suitable for many studies of this kind. The decisions are of course subjective, and, to insure greater objectivity, consultants may be used. The ratings are high, medium, and low.

Marketing: ability of the sales organization to penetrate the market and to establish effective channels and services to handle the new products;

Technology: capability and flexibility of the staff to adapt skills or to acquire the specialized knowledge and expertise necesary to provide back-up for sales and manufacturing;

Production: ability to provide manufacturing management, facilities, raw materials, transportation, and special skills to produce the commodities;

Investment: adequacy of funds to provide for new or modified facilities and working capital.

Preliminary Screening to Select Promising Candidates (Step 5). By scanning Parts A and C of the chart in combination, many sectors can be eliminated at once because they are obviously unattractive or are not at all suited to the capabilities of the organization. Others will stand out as superficially attractive opportunities which should be

Corporate Development

eliminated because of gaps in corporate strengths. Intermediate cases will require greater depth of analysis for decision. It should be borne in mind that some sectors which are not of striking appeal in themselves may yet show very good potential for extending the use of company resources and will therefore be left in the preferred list.

The outcome of this step will be a much shorter array of microsectors which are considered worthy of more serious consideration.

At a later date, when the process is to be repeated in another search for opportunities, it is advisable to make re-evaluations of all sectors by both steps 3 and 4, because in the intervening time the situation may have changed in regard to internal capabilities or in the external economy. This repetition will require less effort than the initial appraisals.

Examination in Depth of Attractive Opportunities (Step 6). The preferred list from step 5 should then be subjected to more searching analysis. The criteria already used in step 3 for defining micro-sector characteristics and in step 4 for determining degree of fit to company resources may be applied again for this step, but the examination should be more thorough and critical. The task force may prefer, however, to reinforce its procedures in order to make its assessments more penetrating. Additional criteria may be added in each case, or a list of four or five gradations in scoring may be employed, in order to reveal more clearly the finer distinctions in attractiveness.

The end result will be a still shorter list of preferred sectors of industry which are believed to be of such relevance to growth plans that they should be submitted to top management for consideration. Because the types of decisions on courses of action vary widely, and these may compete only in part for the same specialized functions, it is not essential that recommendations be made at this time regarding priorities.

Managerial Decisions on Courses of Action (Step 7). Decisions reached by top management for implementation of items in the list from Step 6 may take various forms, of which the following are illustrative:

> **Immediate Implementation:** The opportunity is judged to be so attractive and so well within the company's means, that a program should be started as soon as possible to enter com-

mercial production and sales. At the same time the task force may be asked to make additional studies to clarify some details. By hindsight it is now hard to understand how such an obvious opportunity had been overlooked. Instances of failure to see such promising ventures before systematic analysis was applied are not so rare as one might assume.

Projected Entry by Joint Venture or Merger: The opportunity is very attractive, but, to insure vigorous entry on a commercial scale, it seems desirable to strengthen the internal marketing, technologic, or manufacturing resources by seeking a collaborative undertaking, rather than to follow the slower course of building up these strengths within the organization.

Confirm by Intensive Market Investigation: The outlook is definitely encouraging, but more positive information on sales potential is needed for final decision.

Study Technologic Requirements in Greater Depth: Although the sector holds considerable promise, the technology needs to be explored more thoroughly and therefore a research and development project should be started.

Postpone for Future Consideration.

Drop Consideration, at least for the present time.

CHAPTER EIGHT
TASK FORCES FOR OTHER CORPORATE FUNCTIONS

The preceding chapters have dealt mainly with the use of diversified project teams for new product development and for corporate development to illustrate task force methodology. It is the contention of the author that those techniques can be extended with benefit to the planning, organization, and control of many other business functions. By redefining them as tasks slanted toward bettering performance through injection of a wider scope of expertise, managers would give them a more aggressive posture.

The procedures described in this chapter are all in actual use by some organizations. While the estimation and control of effort, i.e., expenditure of time by participants, are frequently not so rigorous as one might wish, nevertheless, the planning of a collaborative approach is an advance in the right direction. As more attention is devoted to cost-benefit relationships of managerial activities, better scheduling of expertise will surely come about.

Engineering Activities

Engineers were given credit in an earlier section for pioneering the adoption and perfection of the systematic use of task forces. They did this to provide workable solutions for assigned problems and to carry their conclusions through to practice in the form of a completed facility. This concept of group action is introduced in engineering training as early as the undergraduate years, during which experimentation is often carried out by teams of students who plan and coordinate individual functions, the results of which are consolidated in a report. When they later enter employment with the engineering department of a firm or with an independent engineering organization, they readily fall into the established system of project task forces.

Managers of other departments who are attracted to the idea of interdisciplinary approaches have therefore only to turn to their internal engineering associates to see such a scheme in operation; nearly all of them use these principles to carry out their regular duties. Their managerial experience can thus serve as a model for adapting the techniques to other functions. Administrative control of time distribution in engineering departments is usually adequate for proper allocation and costing of professional skills, and their procedures can be adapted to the needs of other departments.

The engineers themselves can assist in promoting the progress of adoption by pulling into their team structures whenever possible representatives of other departments. This movement is made more desirable by the increasing complexity of decision-making.

Major headaches of engineering administrators are brought on by overruns in construction projects. The engineers are usually given the blame. If they can work more closely with top management to develop understanding of cost escalation due to inflation between the date of the original estimate and the postponed decision to go ahead with the facility, life will be less harried for them. Also, if they can point out more forcibly the penalties paid for belated change-orders, they can help their associates to a more realistic attitude in initial analysis of their requirements.

Plant Location Studies

The selection of a site for a new facility is usually assigned as the primary responsibility of manufacturing management. Obviously the decision has to be based on many factors, including the long range plans of top management for the growth of the company.

A summary of the points to be considered is found in the chapter by Leonard C. Yaseen in **Handbook of Business Administration** (Mc-Graw-Hill Book Company, 1967, pages 7/14-7/23). From the check-list which he gives it is seen that inputs are needed from the following additional corporate functions: traffic, personnel, legal, engineering, purchasing, accounting and tax experts. If these aspects are to be evaluated with proper weighting and timing, the organization of a task force is desirable. Otherwise, some specialists may carry out their studies in too great or too little depth to provide optimum impact on the decision. Further, if the parameters of the project have not been subdivided suitably, an after-thought may make necessary an undue amount of reevaluation.

Sometimes special factors come into the picture. For example, the location of a food processing factory requires an analysis of the supply of farm produce in the area, both as to quantity and grade, as well as the possibility of improving this supply. Hence, agronomists and agricultural economists should be added to the team to analyze the means for increasing production to meet manufacturing volume requirements and schedules, and to provide the farmers with incentive to upgrade their husbandry.

Sales and Production Scheduling

Many companies use standing "committees" to make monthly plans for marketing programs and for scheduling their manufacturing operations. These should, and usually do, act as task forces, because they not only make plans on the basis of available information, but also take managerial action to implement the plans. In addition to their regular monthly meetings, they carry out continual interim adjustments to meet changing requirements. The two types of task forces have somewhat different representation of specialists, and of course their decisions must be closely coordinated.

The marketing group has a sales executive as leader, and for necessary coordination the manufacturing department should be represented by a senior member. Other specialists are needed from advertising to tie in the promotional activities, and from traffic to provide a schedule for movement of goods from the plant to the customer. Sometimes the credit manager will be needed for discussion of terms of sale. The result of the meeting will be tentative sales quotas for the period of estimate and often projections still further ahead as general guidelines.

The sales estimates form the basis of planning by the manufacturing group, headed by a production executive and attended also by the representative of the sales department. The manufacturing schedule will of course take into account the inventory situation. Purchasing should supply a team member to make arrangements for raw materials, containers, and supplies. The traffic department should be represented to provide transportation for incoming raw materials and to confirm the schedules for dispatch of products to distribution points.

Changing situations call into action between regular meetings some of the members to take coordinated steps for required alterations in program. Rarely is there any attempt to take into account the time expended on these activities except for the common complaint that everyone spends too much time attending meetings. It is a safe guess that if they were subjected to time-card control, better efficiency would **result.**

Feasibility Studies

Before a prudent executive authorizes a sizable program aimed at a new undertaking, he requires a comprehensive evaluation on which to base his decision. While interest often centers at first on financial aspects, a great many industrial cases involve also a study of the marketing and production situation, and frequently of the technologic background. A significant part of the investigation should be a comparison of the prospects for the idea with those of alternatives available to the company.

A corporate development group, as described in Chapter 7, is a valuable aid in organizing a study of this character, to relieve the burden of senior executives who may be involved in making the final decision. All the needed skills will probably not be available in this staff department, and therefore a task force approach, including representatives from other functions, is an excellent procedure.

Market Development

The operations of the line sales department, although they may be very effective for the regular products of the firm, may prove inadequate for the introduction of innovative new products and services, and still less adequate for entering a new marketing area. In spite of bonuses that may be provided to stimulate sales attention to the innovative product, the pressures of taking care of current business just do not leave enough time for suitable indoctrination into the novel why's and wherefore's of the new product for the systematic nursing that is necessary to secure acceptance by customers.

Various means of filling this gap are used by different companies. In some there is a New Product manager who has innovation as his major responsibility. Others use the product manager concept; these managers are concerned with the regular line but are often supposed to squeeze out enough time to coordinate the efforts of the laboratory, line sales, and promotion and advertising to help along newer members of the product family. Still others use a staff of technical salesmen attached to the sales department, which may also resort for this purpose to borrowing specialists from the laboratory or plant.

Where a corporate development department exists, it may be called upon to diagnose the needs for special sales attention and the best means of organizing the collaboration of different departments. It may

Other Corporate Functions

be asked to take responsibility for managing these activities until the introductory period has been satisfactorily passed, at which time the product can be turned over to the line sales force. The approach may be handled through a group selected from the laboratory, marketing, and advertising.

Any of the above schemes can be productive, depending on the people involved and the communications among them. The main point is that management should take into account the nature of the problems of introducing innovation to the trade and should select the best means of coordinating the inputs of diversified specialists.

Pollution Abatement

The recovery of values from by-products and wastes is always an appealing idea, in addition to its importance for reducing nuisances. Some instances have resulted in spectacular commercial successes. All too often, though, much effort has been wasted because there was inadequate correlation among the laboratory, the plant, and the sales department in evaluating technoeconomic questions. A corporate development group can supply the medium for coordinating these efforts.

Today this subject has greatly increased significance. Public outcry is forcing a much more aggressive attitude on the part of managers to reduce pollution in all its forms. Legal problems arise from stricter regulations. Public relations aspects can have profound effects on the corporate image. As never before stress is being laid on executives to use the best techniques they can devise to give well-rounded solutions. In fact, early in the course of developing a new product or process, an environmental specialist should be used to point out potential pollution hazards, so that the estimated cost of abating them may be included in analyzing economic feasibility.

Technical Audits

Over 20 years ago, Arthur D. Little, Inc., in response to client requests, developed a specialized service for a comprehensive study of the technical needs of an organization as compared with the content of existing programs to supply these services. There exists in many companies a big gap between what the management expects in the way of improved technology and what can reasonably be expected from the research and development effort it is willing to support. The problems arise through failure in communications; unfortunately, there are no quantitative yardsticks ready for supplying data to settle the arguments. The technical audit was designed as an interdisciplinary program to reconcile the views of management and technical directors.

An investigation of this kind can be and often is carried out by an internal task force. There is a severe handicap in organizing such projects in that it is extremely difficult to find executives in the company who are competent and available for this kind of study and who at the same time are free from preconceived biases. As a result of this situation, ADL has been engaged to carry out well over 200 projects of this kind, chiefly for industry but also for quite a number of public agencies. The clients represent a very wide diversity of enterprises, both as to type of business and size. It is very gratifying to me, as one who has participated actively in many of the studies, that the batting average for acceptance and implementation of our recommendations has been remarkably high.

A major problem is the lack of adequate guidance from management (and also of requests from technical directors for this guidance) in regard to growth policies and plans of the company which will provide a framework for an appropriate technical program. A product policy is a definite step in the right direction. Still better is a technical policy, framed jointly by management and technical executives, but such documents are very rare.

A basic misunderstanding on the part of management is the gamut of technical activities which have to be included in the program. The chief executives naively think that most of the work is devoted to glamorous innovations that will produce large profits and sales. These are what we term aggressive projects, but they do not often account for more than 20 percent of the total technical budget, rarely to as much as 40-50 percent, and frequently practically zero, depending on the company and the industry in which it is engaged. The lion's share of the work is on defensive activities, and is the price to be paid for staying competitive in the business. These latter activities include development of related but non-innovative products (new items), product and process improvement, technical service to manufacturing and sales, and assistance in quality maintenance. Together they make up in most cases over 80 percent of the technical budget.

Other Corporate Functions

Other important aspects of a technical audit are examination of technical management procedures, particularly for project definition, justification, organization, execution, and control; communications with management, operating departments, and staff groups; competence in technoeconomic evaluations within the department or obtainable elsewhere in the organization; personnel policies, particularly as they relate to professional development; and mechanisms, in cooperation with operating departments, for moving projects effectively toward commercialization.

Appraisal of technologic institutes in developing countries is an extremely timely subject; in theory they offer a vitally important service for upgrading local technology, but in practice few of them live up to their potential. A comprehensive program for studying their strengths and weaknesses is described in "Industrial Research Institutes: Guidelines for their Evaluation," based on a manuscript by the author, published by the United Nations Industrial Development Organization (1971).

Laboratory Location

In the past 40 years, there has been a strong trend toward locating research and development laboratories on university-type campuses away from metropolitan centers. The choice of site involves many considerations, among which may be listed: accessibility to the executive offices of the company or agency; availability of appropriate housing for the staff; relaxation of zoning restrictions for an operation which may present some over-exaggerated hazards, particularly if pilot plants are included (I favor locating large pilot plants, insofar as possible, adjacent to commercial plants); control of wastes and pollutants; public relations with the community; proximity to a university for professional development of the staff. In some cases, consultants are used to save the time of company executives on these bothersome questions, and experienced architect-contractors are quite frequently used for designing the buildings themselves.

Quality Control

The supervision of quality control has been one of the most backward forms of technical management. It is traditionally carried out by the manufacturing department as a "go/no go" routine, an arrangement which is wrong in principle because no operation should police its own performance. Quality control is being much improved as a result of new instrumentation, new testing methods, and the stricter regulations of public agencies. Then, too, industrial engineers are using the results together with quantification of the flow of materials to carry out weight balance sudies as a means of improving efficiency of operations. Companies with several plants manufacturing the same products may appoint a quality supervisor reporting to a senior executive to maintain product uniformity throughout its markets. This idea is often carried too far in foreign plants, where the objective of world-wide product identity leads to the neglect of the important requiremens of the local market.

Handling of Complaints

Most companies could profit from a broad look at the manner in which complaints about product quality or service are treated. This is usually done on a spot basis, without looking into the significance of the data for improving operations or inspection procedures. Occasionally even the company president gets into the act by handling all complaints personally, when he should assign the responsibility properly and use his time to some better purpose. A very amusing incident happened during World War II when a very high military personage had a pair of shoes obtained from a field depot go all to pieces in two days; the remnants were returned under "secret" classification, and, when the experts finally got access to them, simple inspection of the manufacturer's code showed they had been made in 1916.

Trouble-shooting

Often the privilege of calling on the research laboratory for help on process difficulties is not used intelligently by the manufacturing department. Task forces of operating superintendents, research managers, industrial engineers, and quality controllers could well find that one or two trouble-shooting engineers in the production organization, using the research laboratory as consultants in case of real need, can solve the problems more quickly, cheaply, and satisfactorily.

Accounting Summaries

One of the most logical systems I have seen of summarizing accounting data on a schedule of need-to-know was installed by an industrial engineer turned accountant. Working in a series of task groups with top management, operating managers, and accounting supervisors, he obtained agreement on the content and timing of

Other Corporate Functions

reports to meet the various needs of decision-makers; he organized the complex of inputs of detailed data to conform to the required schedule. He simplified the organization of information so that nonessentials were removed. He adopted the philosophy that no new items should be added to the barebones until their necessity was proved; instead, if a special facet of operations required study, this was done on an ad hoc basis instead of superimposing it on an already heavy load of information.

Reporting Systems

Exactly the same abuses occur in reporting as in accounting, and the remedies are parallel. Some executive becomes irked at a situation, for example, and demands that special reports be added. Instead of treating this as a temporary measure, the reports often become routine. Finally, as a result of the overload of paperwork, the management institutes a survey with the result that a curtailment is effected. Unless watch is maintained, the volume of reporting gradually creeps back again to an undesirable level.

Process Engineering

Unless there is very close interdisciplinary coordination between technologists and development engineers, and between development engineers and the general enginering department, there is likely to be much lost motion between large laboratory scale and piloting, and an even bigger gap between the latter and the engineering of the commercial plant. This difficulty can be alleviated by a task force system. One device I found very useful in carrying a complicated synthesis involving 16 steps from pilot operations to final design was to transfer temporarily the pilot project engineer physically and administratively into central engineering. Instead of having to transfer the large amount of know-how from one group to another, he carried it with him; in effect, therefore, he was acting as a leader of a joint development-engineering collaboration. Being actually in the engineering department for the specific purpose, he enjoyed full cooperation of the staff and the use of all facilities. As a result, the design and installation proceeded smoothly, the operation was carried successfully through the tune-in period, and responsibility was turned over to the production department at design capacity and on schedule.

Market Research on New Products

There is a large gap also between product development technology and market research, particularly when the latter is located in the sales department, with major activity on existing or closely related products and only periodic concern with innovative new products. When requested by technology to forecast the potential for a new product concept, working at arm's length, the study is likely to be carried out in more detail than is warranted at the particular stage, because of faulty communication. This over-doing of preliminary market estimation is encouraged by failure to keep track of costs on individual assignments. For example, a company in the consumer products field will sometimes charge back to the department making the request the expense of consumer testing done by an outside service organization, but will completely ignore the cost of work which it does internally. Another fault may lie in over-extending the size of the internal market research staff and the amount of service built up in other service organizations, with the result that the whole complex chases its tail carrying out elaborate studies on very minor changes of product which are not reflected by the data within the limits of error; after all, consumer testing is not an exact science. When I have pointed this situation out to some receptive clients, I have recommended that these excellent resources for market investigation be oriented instead toward product line diversification, a suggestion which has taken root.

Job Enrichment in Repetitive Tasks (JERT)

The boredom of carrying out a limited range of operations as a routine task has been accentuated by assembly line manufacturing. It is the subject of great complaint among the workers, but little constructive action has been taken until very recently. According to social philosophers, in olden days the joy of being one's own master in planning and conducting work to the end result of an individually completed product gave a sense of deep personal satisfaction which is now lacking. A sceptic may question whether this utopia was shared by all, or whether the long hours of bitter drudgery were the cause of woe to all except those rare people who really loved to work.

Diversification of job content is a logical extension of interdisciplinary principles. For this activity, I propose the acronym JERT, derived from the title of this section.

Other Corporate Functions

From the professional point of view, quality control has been the most dreary of technical operations. The carrying out of routine "go/no go" testing offered little challenge. Workers have sometimes been detected writing down the expected results without bothering to make any actual readings. The situation has been improving, however, in recent years, and the injection of some constructive departure from routine has aroused the interest of all but the most sluggish employees. This has come about through the introduction of more sophisticated test methods and instruments, the correlation of data with complaints, the combination of quality control and production control to improve process performance, and the elevation of responsibility for product quality to a higher executive level.

A very instructive case history of increasing the involvement of all employees in a garment production plant is recounted in **Management by Participation,** by Morrow, Bowers, and Seashore (1967). In the foreword of that book it is noted that integrated efforts were required among accountants, engineers, general managers, and behavioral specialists. The text is chiefly concerned, however, with social science aspects, and interdisciplinary features are implied rather than directly described. By making all the workers conscious of identification with the goal of upgrading the performance of the organization, a marked improvement in efficiency was brought about. To me the pragmatic moral is that, instead of worrying about the theory of the "management of change," a favorite topic of academicians, the simple thing to do is to make the entire staff the agents of change.

Still more recently the use of a team-production method in Swedish automobile plants has been noted (**Time,** January 17, 1972, pp. 58-59). The techniques being investigated are the classical interdisciplinary procedures. Semi-autonomous groups of four to seven workers are given responsibility for assembling certain components; they may be accorded permission to decide in what order to perform their assignments and even to choose their foremen. In other trials the operators move along the line to carry out successive operations or rotate turns at different jobs.

The struggle to overcome "blue-collar blues" is spreading. Efforts in this direction are being made by a number of American companies (**U.S. News & World Report,** April 16, 1973, pp. 121-122). Changes in labor-management practices are being made in several European countries, **(ibid.,** July 23, 1973, pp. 67-78). Lessening of detailed manual operations in office work through the use of computers points to similar opportunities among white-collar employees.

This trend toward job enrichment should be watched closely by all managers. It offers important opportunities for improving morale and productivity. It presents a new challenge to enlightened management to find ways of improving the attitudes and satisfactions of its operators.

The Distribution of Executive Efforts

Brief mention has been made earlier of the lack of efficiency in the way many executives use their time. Their functions are composed of many discrete tasks, some of which they must head themselves, while others they can delegate. They must resist insidious, unimportant pressures in order to concentrate on the essential parts of their jobs. And each set of responsibiilties varies according to the types of obligations imposed and the personnel resources available to share the load.

The natural history of a general executive is an intriguing topic. He normally rises through the organization in a particular area of specialization, although some companies succeed in broadening his interests and skills by a succession of assignments to different departments or by exposure to management training courses. In a great many cases, however, if he has been in sales, he remains the top salesman, if he has been in research he is still his own technical director. Because of his preeminence, he is less likely to build up a strong head for his former area of activity. His bents, his associations, his prestige, his experience conspire to take a disproportionate share of his thinking and time, when he would do better to learn more about other functions he has to oversee.

It is really not all that hard for an executive to plan better deployment of his talents, but who is going to be brave enough to bell the cat? If he will decide himself to make a short list of his major responsibilities, he can propose a logical regime for distribution of his time among them. In setting priorities, he should take into account task force principles by making allowance for potential sharing of the burden with his associates. Certainly there will be emergencies to disrupt his virtuous resolve, but at least he has a plan.

Other Corporate Functions

It is not enough just to outline a program; he needs to check performance. Using the same list of responsibilities, his secretary can make a pretty solid guess as to the content of his schedule, and she may have an interesting private opinion of his efficiency. If he will spend two minutes each day checking her break-down of how his time vanished, a weekly or monthly summary will help him to avoid traps in order to follow the straight road his judgment dictates.

The most obvious way for an executive to subdivide time is according to major departments (sales, manufacturing, technology, finance, or accounting), or according to major commodity or marketing areas, or some combination of the two. Liberal allowance should be included, however, for corporate activities of planning and policy formulation.

Another device for efficiency is to settle early in each meeting, even when only two people are involved, the scope of subjects and probable duration. If this can be done before the session starts, so much the better. To set a good example, I try to prepare in advance short agenda arranged as a priority list, and I recommend the same procedure to my associates.

Analysis of Functional Obligations of an Executive. A better approach to the use of an executive's time is to break down the job content into primary managerial responsibilities, both internal and external. Five of the internal functions are often cited by experts on management theory, viz., planning, organizing, staffing, overseeing, and controlling. To these should be added a sixth, namely, appraising, to emphasize the fact that an efficient manager should continually examine the procedures that have been used for different activities to determine from experience how best similar problems should be handled in the future. Unless this activity is specifically labeled, it is likely to be put off for the future, with the result that it is not done at all.

These six major functions may be suitable as the basis for analyzing the time distribution of an executive in charge of a line operating department or a staff group, disregarding for the moment any effort he may devote to external matters. In planning his program, he is likely to follow a pattern considerably different from a pro rata allocation of one-sixth of his available time to each. Instead, he will vary the relative emphasis according to his judgment as to which types of activities require greater personal attention. Here, too, task force concepts are helpful as a means of considering the possibility of organizing small teams, of which he may act as leader, to carry out the functions in an orderly manner.

To return to the more complex problem of a chief executive's program, he usually has very important external functions in addition to general overseeing of internal activities. His burden is frequently lightened by delegating the inside workings of the organization to one or more deputies, often with the title of executive vice-president, but he is still ultimately responsible for their performance, and must therefore exercise broad surveillance over them.

The major external functions of the chief executive are usually four in number: relations with the Board of Directors, particularly in cases where there are outside members; relations with stockholders in a publicly owned company, or with authorizing agencies in the case of a government operation; liaison, if only to lend prestige, with major customers and suppliers; general public relations, because he is inherently the front man for the organization.

With six internal functions and four external functions, the total of 10 directions in whcih to channel his efforts appears too long to entice most chief executives into budgeting their time. Furthermore, because at that level his responsibiilties are of wide scope, some simplification of his time card is highly desirable.

The six internal functions may be condensed to three as a move in this direction. For example, a natural set of combinations might be: (1) appraising and planning; (2) organizing and staffing; and (3) overseeing and controlling. In all cases, the two components have overlapping features, but using the combined titles is good practice to emphasize the fact that each can be broken down into two functions.

Simplification of the list of four external activities is not quite so easy because different groups of people are involved. The scheme adopted will depend on the particular circumstances. In some instances, relations with the Board of Directors might be combined with stockholder relations, while in others a joint activity for stockholders and the public might be more appropriate. But even if all four were included, the total list of seven, including three composite internal functions, should not be too burdensome for systematic allocation of effort.

Other Corporate Functions

As a final comment, the details of the procedures are not the important thing; the fact that the executive is trying to analyze performance for most effective use of his time is what counts.

Management of Internal Meetings. The waste of managerial time in poorly planned and inefficiently conducted meetings is appalling. Bruce Old, with rare dry humor, wrote a paper a number of years ago "On the Mathematics of Committees, Boards, and Panels" **(The Scientific Monthly, 63, 129-134, 1946).** In mock-serious vein, he analyzed the influence on effectiveness of the number of members, their administrative rank, the characteristics of the chairman, the heckler-saboteur function, and so on. His conclusions: "The lack of correlation achieved in this paper is regretted. It may be that the choice of parameters was completely unsound. One point which particularly baffles the author is the peaking of the efficiency of output of a committee versus number of committee members at seven-tenths of a person. Obviously one must conclude that either further research is required or that people are no damned good."

A simple set of self-evident precautions for running meetings will help the good cause:

1. The participants should be kept to a minimum number on a need-to-be-there basis. Others whose inputs are needed on certain items can be called in for this purpose, preferably on a set schedule so as to interfere least with their other duties.
2. The chairman should act in exemplary manner, maintaining schedule and order of business as closely as possible, avoiding road blocks of lengthy discussions by appointing sub-groups to handle them, and clearly delegating responsibility for action and needed follow-up.
3. Participants should receive sufficient advance notice of schedule, expected attendance, agenda, and back-up papers in condensed form, to encourage preparatory review.
4. Minutes should be kept and distributed promptly.
5. Follow-up on delegated responsibilities should be vigorous.
6. In the case of standing committees, their charters and effectiveness should be reviewed periodically.
7. Separate task groups should be appointed whenever needed to carry out systematic programs in order to recommend solutions for defined problems.

CHAPTER NINE

PROJECTS IN THE PUBLIC DOMAIN

The great increase in the complexity of public questions and undertakings has led to much interest in the use of interdisciplinary principles. Indeed, one of the forces behind this movement is federal legislation; the National Environmental Policy Act explicitly demands the use of interdisciplinary measures for the analysis of environmental impacts and for the consideration of project alternatives. To illustrate the inchoate character of interdisciplinology in public affairs, however, although the Government has set a requirement, it does not define its nature, depth, or components. The state-of-the-art is obviously in the early stages of evolution.

This chapter is therefore devoted to a summary of typical problems, with emphasis on sources of expertise and the roster of needed skills. A more comprehensive discussion will be found in "Power to the States: Mobilizing Public Technology," a 1972 report to The Council of State Governments prepared by a team from Arthur D. Little headed by William D. Carey, Vice President, to whom I am greatly indebted for helpful comments on this entire chapter.

In this presentation, description of the composition of the team is usually limited, to avoid repetition of material in previous chapters, to the team leader responsible for the recommendations, together with mention of other personnel who have been major participants. The reader is referred to earlier chapters for details of the organization and operation of interdisciplinary teams.

Because the projects to be discussed here are defined as being in the public interest, the means of securing a balanced appraisal of the reactions of the general public assumes great importance. The rapid rise of organized pressure groups presents the hazard that their voices may reflect special interests rather than those of the universe of individuals who are affected. This subject is pursued further in the final section of the chapter, with suggestions for greater use of systematic opinion polls, the reliability and credibility of which have been much increased by improved techniques.

Social benefits from public projects are extremely difficult to quantify. As a result, decisions regarding them are often based on the flow and ebb of emotional tides rather than on logic. There is great need for basic thinking to improve the rationale of social values. Political log-rolling, too, is often a self-serving emotional appeal to the electorate which brings about costly deviations from the dictates of reason.

Methodology

The techniques for obtaining effective interlocking of diverse skills have already been described at length; to avoid repetition they will not be discussed again here. The reader is referred for this material to earlier chapters on task forces for product development (Three), task forces for successive stages (Four), administrative control of task forces (Five), task forces for corporate development (Seven), and task forces for other corporate functions (Eight). Also the next three chapters on industrialization programs for developing countries describe procedures for orderly planning of economic development and in this sense are pertinent to projects in the public sector.

The competence of the team leader is vitally important to the success of public projects. His style of operation can make or break the combined efforts of all the other members. Because his abilities are such a critical factor, it is essential that he be chosen on the basis of proved success as a team leader for projects carried out previously. He must be able to hold the team together and orchestrate the individual inputs, bcause otherwise the members are likely to dissipate their efforts in many directions. The managerial rules that apply to effective interdisciplinary collaboration all center in him: constructive and positive leadership, lateral coordination and cross-briefings, conflict resolution, feed-back and feed-forward of information, correction of initial strategies, and disciplined and timely reporting governed by the communications network he has established.

The physical arrangements for housing the nucleus of team activities is more important than one might assume. Much of the work of the members may be done in their regular locations, because there they have the advantages of information files, selected reference books, and, particularly, proximity to colleagues on whom they may call for advice or collaboration. But cross-coordination is the essence of effective task force operations. Therefore they should have a central location with facilities for meetings and individual desk space. If they do not need to use their regular offices for the reasons mentioned

Public Projects

above, they should spend their working time in the central headquarters. In spite of great advances in aids to physical means of communications—telephones, intercoms, easy reproduction of written material, and the like—these cannot take the place of the give-and-take of face-to-face discussions.

Operations Research in Public Projects. Because of the number and complexity of variables, the techniques of operations research are particularly important among the skills needed for problem solving in the public domain.

John F. Magee states that (private communication): "OR and its cousin (or child) Systems Analysis made and can make major contributions to public projects. (Systems analysis is the conceptual study of proposed complex systems, while operations research tends to be the experimental and analytical study of real systems in being.) For example:

> "Construction: OR people developed the concepts of critical path scheduling, PERT and other forms of network analyses to aid in construction project management.
>
> Water utilization: One of the early outstanding books in the OR field was focused on the economics and cost-benefit analysis of water utilization (Roland N. McKean, **Efficiency in Government through Systems Analysis, with Emphasis on Water Resources Development**, 1958).
>
> Police and Fire Protection: The RAND Corporation, for example, has been working on these areas for the City of New York.
>
> Transportation systems: This has been an important area for systems analysis and operations research—traffic control, rates, scheduling, equipment selection, etc. The ADL-OR group has done a lot in this area as have others."

Sources of Diversified Expertise

The complexity of the problems may require a variety of skills not available in the agencies which have responsibility for the studies. To supplement their personnel resources they often either borrow specialists from other departments or transfer them temporarily to their own control. Both methods have advantages and disadvantages which will be discussed below.

In considering how to assemble the team, the requirements for optimum performance should be kept firmly in mind. First, the selected individuals should be free to act on their own responsibility without being subjected to supervision from higher administrative levels. Second, they should have a common assembly point, as mentioned earlier, to promote intimate face-to-face interaction with other participants.

The borrowing of personnel often results in a collection of individuals who have not had the experience of working in a composite team. Hence they must be indoctrinated in the theory and practice of how to perform their respective roles most effectively, a situation which adds to the duration and cost of the operation. That this is not a fast or easy process is illustrated by the discussion in the appendix, "How to Start Interdisciplinary Systems."

Borrowing of personnel from other departments on an ad hoc, part-time basis tends to remove them from domination by administrative superiors in their own organizations, but this freedom is not necessarily the case. On the other hand, the requisite degree of freedom in scheduling their participation may be in conflict with their regular duties, a situation which is sometimes aggravated by hostility of a superior to loss of control over disengaged activities.

Transfer of personnel to a new administrative relationship has the advantage of removing them from the jurisdiction of their regular line superiors. But the use of their time may not be efficient or economical, because, my own experience shows, the efforts of participants are most advantageously used on a flexible, part-time schedule.

To obtain greater objectivity, efficiency, and a wider range of skills, public agencies are turning increasingly to outside consulting organizations, particularly for planning and evaluation. They are able to offer teams, composed of individuals of varied expertise, with less prior exposure to built-in prejudices, who are accustomed to working together in an interdisciplinary climate. The cost of outside services is sometimes an obstacle, just as it is in the case of clients from private industry, because the proposals are compared with estimates of carrying out the work in-house, in which the true total expense is often not reflected because fringe benefits and full overheads are not included. Furthermore, overruns of internal estimates are quite common experience, and are accepted usually without much uproar, whereas a consultant is committed to living within the budget of his proposal unless additional sums are allocated by renegotiation because of change in scope of the investigation.

Public Projects

When consultants are used, there may be a chasm between formal acceptance of the findings and recommendations and actual use. Therefore the public client should give much weight to the question of what he is going to do with the report when he gets it. Because this is not done in many cases, the files of government agencies are overflowing with consultant reports which have not been, and probably never will be, implemented. It is not the consultant's fault; it is a failure of the management process to build assurances of acceptability into the arrangements.

Essentials in Relationship with Consultants

My philosophy of how best to meet the mutual responsibility between consultant and client is an endeavor to overcome the problem of making sure that the recommendations are useful. This involves six major points, which are discussed further below. They apply equally to the relations of consultants to clients in the private sector.

(1) Is the assignment justified as defined?

(2) Does the program as a whole conform to the terms of the agreement?

(3) Has the client been made to understand his own responsibility?

(4) Has the client been kept adequately abreast of the progress of the work?

(5) Are the findings and recommendations in most acceptable form for consideration and implementation?

(6) Is the report constructive in tenor, without unnecessary overtones of destructive criticism?

Although this discussion is framed in terms of consultant-client relationships, the same precautions apply equally to internal professional studies. The results are often not assessed in the same rigorous manner in the case of an in-house project unless there is some form of contractual agreement. To assure proper recognition of staff capabilities as a resource, however, the same basic principles should govern the appraisal of investigations carried out within the organization.

Validity of the Assignment. It is common experience in consultancy that the client may ask for the wrong thing. The vital question is, of course, will the results be useful in solving the problem? An essential part of the consultant's obligation is to make an objective analysis of the client's need. The latter too often, like the user of home remedies, mistakes the superficial symptoms for the true cause. Only by delving beneath the initial inquiry can a proper course of investigation be proposed. This can be a hardship on a consultant who is hungry for work, but in the long run it pays off to refuse an unproductive assignment; the lion's share of a consulting practice comes from repeat requests by satisfied clients. Gossip about unsuccessful engagements, however, seems to fly about much faster than the news of successful projects.

Conformance of Program with Assignment. A consultant should review periodically the terms of the agreement with the client to make sure that the program conforms with the letter and spirit of his obligation. In enthusiasm for following new ideas, he may unconsciously depart from what he agreed to do. If the divergence is substantive, it should be discussed with the client as soon as possible to solicit his concurrence, particularly if it involves a change in schedule, cost of the project, or policy issues. One of the surest ways to cause trouble in relationships is to diverge from the terms of the agreement.

Mutuality of Objective. There must be a clear understanding that consultant and client are aiming at the same objectives, but the former must retain full professional responsibility for what he does and how he does it. A wise precaution is to establish clearly the individuals who serve respectively as the consultant's team leader and his counterpart in the client's organization. The establishment of a cooperative relationship to reach a common goal must include both policy-making executives and employees at the working level. At the start of the project the sponsoring executive in the client organization should make a suitable internal announcement to those of his associates who will be involved regarding the nature, program, and objective of the assignment. Unless all concerned are made to feel they are partners in the undertaking, the chances of successful problem solving and implementation are much reduced. This policy has the added advantage that some elements of the recommendations may be put into operation before the study has been completed.

Liaison with Client. A consultant in pursuing his program may err in taking it for granted that the client understands he is hard at work, particularly where the chain of direct contact is broken because the assignment involves seeking external sources of information.

Public Projects

When there is full understanding and confidence between the chief representatives of the two parties, this may be the case, but it is advisable for the team leader of the consultant to carry out a regular schedule of contacts with his opposite number. For projects of medium or long duration, a contact at least once a month by personal call, telephone, or letter is a safe rule. These exchanges provide an opportunity for mutual reassurance that there have been no important changes in policy, objectives, or interest on either side.

Character of Report. The report should obviously be in most suitable form for the client's use, although the consultant retains full responsibility for the factual background and recommendations. This is therefore not a question of what is said, but of how it is said. To this end, I prefer to make a preliminary oral report to the client, sometimes at two or more levels in his organization, to present the outline of the findings and recommendations, without any written material except a bare list of subjects. Somehow or other preliminary reports in writing, which are later modified, when left in a client's hands sometimes rise up to haunt one, no matter how they are labeled.

The oral presentation has two objectives:

(1) review of the factual background to make sure that it is correct and complete;

(2) discussion of the manner in which recommendations are to be presented, without necessarily disclosing them in full at the time, so that they will be most useful to the client.

To repeat, the consultant is fully responsible for the final report, but preliminary review gives him an opportunity to make sure that his facts are unquestioned and that his recommendations will be acceptable as practical procedures.

Constructive vs. Destructive Approach. My experience points to the very real advantage of framing the report in positive terms rather than dwelling on the negative features of the present situation. The latter attitude induces resistance and rationalization regarding past practices. As a result, implementation of the proposed changes is made more difficult, because of sullen acceptance of new procedures under pressure.

Examples of Public Projects

Building Construction. The implementation stage for public or housing structures is normally the responsibility of construction engineers or, more commonly in some European countries, architectural engineers who have responsibility to carry through from design to completion. Other skills which may be involved in planning phases, and to greater or less extent in implementation, are expertise in community and public relations, cost-benefit analysis, design of space utilization and auxiliary facilities, environmental protection, legal restrictions, residential accommodations, supply of utilities, transportation facilities, and the like. A mistake that is sometimes made in planning public buildings is to get present staff members heavily involved in planning their own particular facilities; this not only detracts from the general utility of the structure for the future, but also causes a severe disruption of normal activities of the staff.

Dams and Water Utilization, including irrigation systems. The make-up of teams is similar to that given under building construction, plus the skills of agricultural engineers and agronomists for irrigation systems, and power plant specialists for hydro-electric facilities. Prime responsibility for installation rests with construction engineers. Because of the isolated locations of many of these undertakings, some of the disciplines mentioned in the first example play less significant roles.

Economic Development. Many countries and regions undertake systematic programs for improving their economic environment. The methodology for industrial development studies is covered in detail in Chapters Ten, Eleven, and Twelve, with special reference to developing countries. The methodology described is applicable to other situations, with suitable modification of the criteria. Expansion of commerce and trade requires interaction among agencies of government, chambers of commerce, information services, market research and development functions, standardization organizations, and transportation complexes. Development of tourism rests on cooperation among government bureaus, housing groups, public relations and information services, recreational and cultural facilities, and transportation.

Educational Systems. Prime responsibility is assigned to specialists in education, with inputs from specialists in communications, community relations, engineering, finance, library science, and psychology, together with representatives of parents, students, and teachers.

Public Projects

Legislative Procedures. Legislators are turning more and more to the assistance of professional staffs in carrying out their duties. Their needs for staff expertise are in legal research, appropriate technical disciplines, communications, opinion research, public relations, and taxation and finance. They are also using outside sources of opinion to assist them in evaluating the impact of measures they propose.

Police and Fire Protection. The implementation of new procedures is of course the responsibility of civic executives of these services. To aid them in selecting and developing the necessary techniques and equipment, they may call on the assistance of diverse disciplines, depending on the particular case, such as the behavioral sciences, communications, engineering of various types, legal expertise, statistical analysis, systems engineering, training methodology, technology, and transportation.

Pollution Abatement. Environmental specialists make a major input, but the installing and enforcing functions are provided by public agencies. The gamut of assisting disciplines resembles that cited for police and fire protection.

Public Health. With the greatly increased attention being paid to the quality and availability of health services, many systematic appraisals are being made of means of improving medical care. Many new interdisciplinary activities have been stimulated, such as joint surgical-engineering teams to improve diagnostic instruments and prosthetic devices. The broad projects are necessarily headed by members of the public health or medical professions. They demand collaboration of a wide range of specialized personnel for solution. The positive results in the form of improved human welfare offer a high reward of satisfaction to the participants.

Public Utilities. The planning, installation, and operation of facilities for providing public utilities, in either the private or public sectors, are a special aspect of building construction and the pattern of interdisciplinology is similar.

Recreation Facilities. The planning and organization of recreation facilities are primarily the responsibility of bureaus or commissions in government agencies. They make use of conventional forms of expertise, supplemented by such specialists as experts in entertainment and sports.

Statistics and Information Services. Public agencies all over the world are increasing their programs for collection and dissemination of statistical information, which has been greatly aided by advances in statistical techniques and the introduction of computers. The opportunities for collecting data have become so much broader that the current danger is in overworking the respondents, particularly the general public and smaller enterprises. More emphasis should be placed on the relevance of the programs to practical utility, rather than data collection as an end in itself.

Transportation Systems, including highways, waterways, port facilities, airports, and navigation aids. These all represent special aspects of engineering planning and construction, aided by a wide range of physical and social sciences. In regard to the planning of port installations, for example, advances in materials handling necessitate such features as allowing for the different shore area requirements of containerized versus break-bulk cargo, and the special quarantine provisions for free ports to encourage the entrepot function for duty-free processing of materials in transit.

Urban Renewal. The revivification of city centers is headed by civic planners. They call on the assistance of a wide range of specialists in architectural design, behavioral sciences, economics, recreation, system engineering, and transportation.

Welfare. Programs to take care of the needy, in earlier times largely left to private philanthropy, are the subject of many wrangles between spokesmen for the poor and the tax-paying public, who decry the abuses which come to light. Nevertheless, real progress is being made in defining the levels of income necessary for dignified living. The search for more effective ways to supply supplementary benefits continues to remain at stage center, with interdisciplinary approaches to attain equitable, humanitarian distribution.

Public Technology

Mention was made at the beginning of this chapter of the Arthur D. Little report "Power to the States: Mobilizing Public Technology" (The Council of State Governments, 1972), the result of a project sponsored by the National Science Foundation. This document is of such importance to the subject that some aspects will be reviewed briefly here.

Public Projects

A comprehensive tabulation has been made, using a classification into 21 program categories of "Technology Related General Bills," passed by 20 state governments in 1968 and 1970. In 1968 there were 1,454 bills covering 1,250 programs, and in 1970, 1,440 bills in 725 programs. "In some states the output of technology-related legislation was as high as 17 percent. . . . not far removed from informed estimates of Congressional legislation in technology-related fields of 20 to 30 percent. But the qualitative difference between Congressional and state legislative performance may be another matter, considering the comparatively superior research and analytical resources available to the Congress, including standby services of the National Academies of Sciences and Engineering."

The first point in the Digest of Findings is well worth repeating as an exhortation to competent investigation of proposed public undertakings: "The central finding of this study is that state governments have a growing need for 'public technology'—that is, for technological innovation matched to user needs. A very high priority should be given to the implementation of effective delivery systems for bringing public technology to bear in problem solving. If new technology is to meet the needs of the state governments, it must demonstrate utility and payoff. It must be focused on the **users**. It must be deliverable, workable, and affordable. It must respond to the short reaction times of state governments. It must **satisfy**."

Techniques to Obtain a Consensus of Public Opinion

We really have not progressed very far in nearly 2,400 years from the boisterous public assemblies of the citizenry of Athens and other city-states of Greece. One major stride forward was the codification of procedures in deliberative bodies by Rules of Order.

Frequently public projects have moved very far along the road toward implementation before the public gets a chance to voice opinion in public hearings. These often take on a circus aspect because proponents of differing points of view have had a long time to case-harden their adversary postures.

Heretofore, attempts to obtain the sense of the general public have been centered either in obtaining the views of individuals who supposedly represent the average man, through testimony at public hearings, or by the process of referendum on financial support for proposed programs. Both methods have great weaknesses. In the selection of the average man, an "amateur anthropologist" as one of my colleagues dubbed him, we must be very fortunate to secure an individual who truly represents the middle road. A not very satisfactory alternative is to try to reach consensus by throwing two men of widely different opinions into the ring with a moderator. Testimony at public hearings is very often a free-for-all for the airing of the contentions of pressure groups; the vast majority of the citizens, who become organized only under the stress of widespread dissatisfaction, remain silent. The process of the referendum is time-consuming and costly, because much expensive effort has gone into the preparation of the proposal; the validity of the results may be questioned because of voter apathy on the part of all but vigorous proponents and opponents.

The Merits of Expert Opinion Polling. To my mind, the progress in systematic sampling techniques and in the framing of objective questionnaires offers an avenue in tune with the modern spirit of fact-finding. My experience has been largely in information polling on specific professional questions, but I have profound confidence in the ability of pollsters to widen their horizons. Weight is given to this opinion by the growing reliance on the validity of the results of opinion polls and the indirect but often strong effect they have had on the framing of public policies. They offer the additional advantage of being relatively inexpensive, because up-to-date sampling techniques give assurance that test groups of workable size provide answers, within the allowable limits of error, representative of the large universe from which they are selected.

It is my suggestion, therefore, that important public questions, before too much time is spent in debate with little positive effect to show for it, be turned over to pollsters for evaluation of the opinions of those who will feel the impact of the programs, as an integral part of the total study. Unintentional bias in the questionnaires could be corrected by discussion with interested groups, but even here there is often severe disagreement to be reconciled.

In cases where acquisition of real property or rights-of-way is involved, it can be argued that premature disclosure of the project could cause speculative changes in value, but this seems to occur anyway through leaks of supposedly confidential knowledge. Does the public really care all that much whether profiteering is done by a shrewd outsider or by a crony of an insider? The effect could be

Public Projects

reduced in local projects by including distant localities in the inquiry, with keyed codes to permit easy sorting. Or, the exercise of eminent domain might be strengthened to provide for acquisition at reasonable costs. Finally, a pollster might be able to mask the purpose by including the pertinent questions in a broader survey.

The results of such polls would provide a sounder basis for decision-making by public agencies. The size of the opposition and the nature of their disagreement would indicate the precautions that should be taken to safeguard the interests of those in the minority.

Sebastian Chamfort, a prominent figure in the French Revolution, wrote two centuries ago: "The public! How many fools does it take to make a public?" His pessimism has been shared by many other cynics. But the world-wide rise in the level of education has earned the citizenry a right to a more direct voice in framing the rules by which they live.

CHAPTER TEN

THE ENVIRONMENT FOR INDUSTRIAL EXPANSION

Systematic planning of a program of industrial development for a region or a nation requires a realistic frame of reference. This is, so to speak, the infra-structure for charting the proposed directions and rate of growth of the manufacturing sector. Description of the background in developing countries is the aim of this chapter. The two following chapters will be devoted to methodology for selecting and promoting the most promising development opportunities. The process as a whole parallels that described in Chapter Seven, "Task Forces for Corporate Development."

The first step is to create a strong focus in the government structure for framing policies, plans and programs; this is achieved by setting up or strengthening an appropriate organization, such as a ministry or department of industry. Next, factual knowledge of the existing situation, preferably showing historical trends, must be provided to reveal what has occurred without the stimulus of a concerted effort; the data are collected through some form of industrial census. Then an appraisal should be made of the human and material resources of the region or country to insure practicality of the program in a particular economy. Finally, a tentative gross plan for a specified period should be formulated, to be subjected to adjustment and refinement in the light of the findings of the detailed studies to be described later.

In developing countries, and indeed in some mature economies, these subjects are entrusted solely to economists performing the function of national planners. Their skills are of course vitally important for this purpose, but their conclusions become more practical and workable when they are reenforced by the inputs of entrepreneurial management, the financial community, and particularly technologic expertise. Some of the required supplementary skills can be provided by public servants in other agencies, but it is highly desirable to strengthen them with the advisory assistance of leading practitioners of those specialties who are directly concerned with operations on the firing line of business.

Throughout these three chapters the use of interdisciplinary principles is to be understood although this fact will be emphasized specifically only in certain cases where some further explanation appears to be desirable.

Provision of a Government Focus for Industrial Development

In many industrialized countries it has been deemed advisable to set up a separate ministry or department to nurture the growth of the manufacuring sector. In a few cases, however, such as the U.S., a lusty industrial complex has already existed before much attention was being given to the theory and practice of economic development; in these nations, it has been tacitly assumed that no special agency at the national level is needed. Any required services are provided through various other agencies without collecting them under a single structure. Developing countries in general are following the patterns of the majority of mature economies by creating ministries of industry.

Two developing countries with which I am particularly acquainted —Lebanon and Singapore—present an unusual situation in that they had a long history of serving as dominant trading centers in their regions, but, because of limited arable land, had not developed an important agricultural base, in contrast to the situation in a great many developing countries in which this is the major source of employment and production. Both nations wished to expand their manufacturing sectors as a means of increasing their Gross National Product, and particularly to create increased employment to assist in supporting their social goals. Singapore installed a strong development board a number of years ago with the prime objective of stimulating industrial growth. Lebanon relied on a ministry which dealt with the interests of both commerce and industry, but the much greater strength of commerce dominated its programs; steps are now being taken to establish a separate ministry of industry which should prove to be productive of an increased rate of industrial growth.

Government Measures to Stimulate Industrial Development

A number of measures which governments may use to stimulate growth of the industrial sector are listed in the following sections. Most of them require direct action, but some may best be implemented in part through quasi-public agencies or through trade or professional organizations—for example, standardization. To secure broad vision in formulating and carrying out the programs, interdisciplinary teams are advisable, including representation of the views of business managers, financial experts, and practicing engineers and technologists.

Appraisal of National Resources for Development. It has been emphasized previously that, for sound planning and programming, proposed projects should be developed with careful adjustment to the human and material resources of the community which can be brought to bear to achieve the planned goals. The resources can be defined under six headings: managerial, technologic, manufacturing, marketing, regulative, and financial. They will be discussed briefly in this order in the following paragraphs. It should be noted that they parallel those listed for corporate development.

Managerial competence: breadth and depth of managerial expertise, use of management development programs, opportunities for advancement, freedom from organizational or cultural hindrances to good management procedures.

Technology: quality of technical management, attitude of industrial managers toward the application of new technology, availability of competent technologists, educational facilities, organizations to encourage professional development, personnel practices for engineers and applied scientists, institutions and organizations for providing special technical services, conditions affecting the inflow of foreign technology, patent system.

Manufacturing: availability of competent production managers, condition and flexibility of plant equipment, transportation system for raw materials and products, raw material resources, services for replacement or repair of equipment, regulations concerning importation of equipment and raw materials, availability of workers and rate of turnover, training programs for workers, regulations concerning conditions of employment.

Marketing: character of marketing skills and management, quality of market information, composition of markets, distribution systems, state of competition, competition from publicly owned corporations, quality of middlemen in marketing chain, sales training programs, effectiveness of trade associations, trade practices for mark-ups and allowances, credit situation.

Regulatory situation: character of regulations affecting trade and manufacture, stability of regulatory practices, control mechanisms, legal procedures regarding infractions.

Financial factors: availability of capital for commercial loans and industrial investment, practices of development banks and commercial banks, interest rates, opportunities for securing foreign capital, markets for industrial securities, general character of capital formation.

Statistical Information. Most mature economies have developed extensive statistics which are very helpful to industrial entrepreneurs in managing their affairs and in evaluating new opportunities. The data include not only national production data, but also those for domestic markets and foreign trade. Trade associations and financial institutions can be helpful sources of advice to supplement the information collected by government agencies.

Most developing countries have instituted programs for assembling data about their economies. These are very spotty in character, some quite good but others very deficient. Slowness in releasing findings and failure to try out questionnaires on selected samples of respondees are frequent complaints, but these are often true also in advanced countries. The development of computers has accelerated the trend. The contacts with industry in carrying out an industrial census are laborious, because they generally require one or more personal calls by trained interviewers to assist the managers in preparing their responses, particularly in smaller firms, whereas in advanced countries mailed questionnaires are commonly satisfactory. During 1954-55 in Iraq a comprehensive development study by an interdisciplinary team (of which I was the first leader) was greatly aided by preliminary data from the first industrial census which was just being completed. In Lebanon an industrial census was carried out in 1965 and a second was being designed late in 1971, at the time I was making a survey there.

One hazard in collecting information by census is that the designers of questionnaires in their enthusiasm are inclined to ask for more and more data. It is surprising to find in developing countries such a willingness on the part of industrial managers, particularly in small enterprises, to respond to the great detail of the questions which are posed. This happens in advanced countries, too, until the burden becomes so heavy that public clamor arises. A test that should be applied in

Environment For Industrial Growth

the design of questionnaires is to require reasonable proof of the utility of items of requested data before they are approved by the responsible directors.

Framing Industrial Development Policies and Programs

It is becoming a common and constructive practice among nations to adopt an economic development policy, including the industrial sector, for a period of a few years ahead. These policies cover in general terms such subjects as the desired total rate of growth, the break-down with respect to major segments of the economy, the general objectives and character of the proposed expansion, the creation of bodies to implement the plan, and the nature of the assistance which the government will lend in implementation.

When first formulated, these policies are likely to be tinged with wishful desires rather than careful analysis of reasonable goals. Before short-falls in performance become too painful to alibi, the politic remedy is to announce a new policy with improved resemblance to reality.

The statements of general policy are often supplemented by more detailed presentations of programs. These may start with an expansion and clarification of objectives. They may define in one or more lists the preferred micro-sectors of industry to be encouraged (as in Thailand, for instance) with different priority ratings; those not included in the listings are left to the discretion of the private entrepreneur. (In Japan, for example, the major development objectives were in four phases: (1) improvement in the industrial infra-structure; (2) establishment of primary raw material enterprises; (3) encouragement of secondary industries to use these materials; and (4) stimulation of manufactures for export markets). They may give in more detail the measures of support which the government proposes to make available. They may describe the organizations and institutions which are to be invigorated to assist industry. They may cover the regulations governing relations with foreign sources of capital and expertise in technology.

Policies for Technology

Many developing countries, following the example of Western Europe, are formulating policies for science or for science and technology. There is generally, unfortunately, a lack of understanding of the difference between science and technology, and of the fact that in most cases there is no linear relationship between the creation of new scientific knowledge and its practical application; basic scientific research may require many, many years to bear fruit. The bodies which frame these policies are very often heavily dominated by representatives of the academic community, and the voice of technology is at best muted or directed largely at applied research of exotic character which does not meet the present needs of industry, particularly the smaller firms. This statement does not in any way imply that basic research and advanced educational programs should be neglected; it is instead a plea for much greater emphasis on the down-to-earth technical activities that will be of immediate help to improve manufacturing operations.

Policies for technology should, in my opinion, be separately treated from those for science, either by themselves or as a separate section when the two types are combined in one statement. These policy statements, and the more detailed program descriptions that may be used to supplement them, usually start with exhortatory comments about the importance of technology to the nation. They may then set goals, on a time scale, for the levels of financial support for technical activities in public and quasi-public agencies, and also in the private industrial sector. They may define specifically the types of agencies they propose to stimulate, such as government laboratories; autonomous technologic institutes; information and technical service programs to help small enterprise; training courses in technical management; trainee programs to permit acquisition of new professional skills; systematic surveys of national technical resources, including analyses of supply and demand for specialists, to help guide educational programs; and means of encouraging the inflow of foreign know-how. They should, but seldom do, emphasize the development of local skills in technoeconomic evaluations to assist entrepreneurs in appraising proposed new industrial undertakings. They may end up by pointing out specific provisions for support to encourage the private sector to make better use of technology, such as development loans or subsidies, partial support of technical programs, relaxation of taxes to stimulate innovation, and more liberal terms for imports of equipment and materials.

Environment For Industrial Growth

Government Measures to Strengthen Development Resources

This section gives a comprehensive list of means that can be used by government to stimulate industrial development. Their application in practice is illustrated in Chapter Twelve. There is some duplication here, for the sake of completeness, of points mentioned in the preceding section. The discussion should be useful even in advanced countries as a check-list of options for their own public programs.

Investment Climate. Entrepreneurs are deterred by political instability and by uncertainties about legislation affecting company operations and the winning of mineral raw materials. When an influx of foreign capital and expertise is desired, these considerations are particularly important as a means of securing cooperation from abroad.

Management Development. A strong managerial cadre for technology, as well as for other executive functions, is very necessary, and hence stimulation of training programs is highly desirable. In Egypt, for example, the Institute of Management Development, which has been operating for many years as an agency of the U.A.R. Government, has a three-pronged program consisting of training courses, consultation services to individual enterprises (which produce practical case histories for use in training), and comprehensive research on major industrial problems. It has opened its doors to representatives of other Arab countries.

The improvement of managerial skills through so-called Productivity Centers meets with mixed reactions. Some programs I have seen are very beneficial. In other countries they are reputed to be wasted efforts. Much depends on proper orientation of the programs to the cultural characteristics of the host country.

There is much discussion of what makes a good entrepreneur. Is it possible to impart the necessary skills by training? Thus far the consensus seems to be that the traits are largely individual characteristics, but nevertheless subject to improvement by proper training.

A related subject is the provision of training programs for workers and skilled technicians of sub-professional status. The programs in many countries are very effective, although too liimted in scope. The facilities and budgets of these institutions are often the envy of technologic institutes which struggle to find support for activities to provide technical help to industry.

Technologic Institutes. Autonomous, multi-purpose contract research organizations, often called "industrial research institutes" but more fittingly "technologic institutes," are potentially, in my opinion, one of the most effective agencies for supplying new and improved technology to industry. A number have been set up in developing countries in the last two decades, modeled on the American concept, but only in relatively few cases have they expanded their programs adequately. Their lack of success is due to unrealistic expectations; preoccupation with longer range applied research as contrasted with less glamorous but practical technical services; bureaucratic restrictions which have hampered the retention of adequate staff; omission from their skills of technoeconomic capabilities; and inadequate policing of in-house activities to insure relevance to the needs of industry. They cannot be expected to become wholly self-supporting, like their American counterparts, until a robust complex of industry has been built up. They require continuing subsidy from public or quasi-public sources, particularly for information and technical services to small enterprises. They should become a key bridge for the adaptation of foreign technology to local conditions.

Development Financing. An essential factor in industrial development is the availability of capital, which is in short supply in most developing countries. A study of the mechanism of capital formation includes estimation of private savings, plough-back of earnings by industrial enterprises, and accumulation of monies in the public coffers. Any deficiency in the total of these three, as compared with forecasts of the amounts needed to sustain the planned rates of growth, must be obtained from foreign sources or international development agencies. To secure funds from them, the government must put the national house in order to justify their requests.

The functioning of development banks deserves scrutiny. All too often, instead of providing a revolving fund for diversified loans, they freeze their portfolios into a pattern of successful ventures, which they do not wish to shed because of their favorable effect on balance sheets, and of cats and dogs which they are unable to liquidate.

One useful technique in selecting industrial micro-sectors for preferential stimulation is to take into account the range of average capital investment required to provide one additional job opportunity. Where the data are available, the figures may be obtained by dividing

Environment For Industrial Growth

the total capitalization of the micro-sector by the total number of employees. The results need further examination, however, because some capital-intensive installations, such as basic metal winning and petrochemicals, exert a multiplier effect through creation of secondary satellite industries which are based on these raw materials.

Development financing includes such matters as subsidies for start-up expenses or long-term support for particularly desirable micro-sectors.

Market Information: Industrial development is aided by providing fuller information from government sources on domestic markets and export opportunities. The latter may be reenforced by trade agreements and export subsidies.

Protection Against Imports. Protective tariffs and restrictions should be used with discretion; if overdone they may lull the protected operations into complacence, with the net result of a strain on the total economy through public support of high priced products.

Anti-dumping regulations may be needed, including investigation of hidden subsidies used by some countries to manipulate their own economies. Policing of the quality and utility of some imports may be necessary to insure fair competition for local products. Under this heading should be mentioned also the scrutiny of import duties and bureaucratic delay in the securing of raw materials and equipment; inequities sometimes creep in, such as lower duties on semi-manufactures than on raw materials, a situation which impedes the establishment of local processing.

Government Promotional Activities

The procedures described in the preceding section may be carried out quite thoroughly, but the program may still fail to arouse much interest among the entrepreneurial community. To arouse their positive participation, certain educational and promotional steps are necessary to convert generalizations into a display of specific opportunities in a form which is convincing to them. This section presents brief descriptions of the chief types that can be used.

Publicity: It is not enough to have a file of industrial opportunities available for inspection by entrepreneurs. Instead, the message must be carried directly to them by all available channels of communication, and the process must be a continuing effort. It includes stories in newspapers, trade and business publications, general interest magazines, and of course radio and television. It involves personal appearances by government and community leaders before business audiences to endorse and explain the program. It may be extended through discussion groups and seminars. The publicity becomes more telling when current case histories of new undertakings are incorporated as fast as they become available.

Trade Fairs: Many communities have organized trade fairs to illustrate opportunities by display material. These may be used to arouse local businessmen and to attract the interest of foreign entrepreneurs. There is much information available to facilitate planning such affairs, and various international agencies are willing to lend advisory help.

Official Recognition of New Ventures: While one is inclined to think primarily of the profit motive as the incentive for entrepreneurship, the prestige of some form of official recognition should not be overlooked. This may be carried out through public awards of certificates and emblems, either with or without cash prizes, or by membership in honorary orders. Mature countries have found such measures productive, particularly during critical economic conditions or times of war.

Pre-investment Prospectuses: A very telling mechanism for promotional activities is the preparation of illustrative pre-investment prospectuses. These should be written up to describe typical individual opportunities in the form to which investors are accustomed.

CHAPTER ELEVEN
A SYSTEMS APPROACH TO ECONOMIC DEVELOPMENT

The methodology recommended in this chapter is a systematic approach to the selection and appraisal of development opportunities. It is obviously a great improvement over haphazard choices based on arbitrary personal opinions which reflect the biases of individual decision makers. It has the additional advantages of making easier the comparison of alternatives, and of bringing to light overlooked possibilities.

The techniques, adapted from those perfected in corporate development studies, have been proved out in application to the needs of developing countries. A specific case history is described at the end of the chapter to demonstrate practicality.

The methodology can obviously be used for all other major sectors of the economy, such as agriculture, banking and finance, commerce (both internal and foreign trade), communications, construction industries, fisheries, forestry, government operations, mining, tourism, transportation, and utilities (production and distribution). In each case the operations may be broken down into micro-sectors which can be evaluated in terms of both general technoeconomic characteristics and attractiveness in the national environment. Although the present chapter deals with the manufacturing sector, the basic techniques can readily be modified to fit the needs of these other types of activity. The final section of methodology illustrates the method of fitting the development plan for all major sectors into the master plan for the total economy.

Methodology

The methodology involves the following successive steps, which are discussed in detail in later sections of this chapter.

1. Compilation of an array of industrial micro-sectors, grouped under major sector headings, believed to show promise for development; the subdivision into micro-sectors should be sufficiently fine to secure reasonable technoeconomic homogeneity;
2. Selection and definition of criteria—using interdisciplinary teams of development economists, technologists, process engineers, and

market researchers—to evaluate (a) general characteristics of the micro-sectors, and (b) degree to fit to the internal resources of the country;

3. Independent and parallel scoring of the array of micro-sectors by interdisciplinary teams—using a simple scoring system of high, medium, and low—to permit selection by inspection of those which show most attractive potential for the economy;

4. In the next step, more incisive appraisal, using stricter criteria, of the survivors of the screening process to make final selection of a list of opportunities for further consideration;

5. Examination of the final list of micro-sectors to reach decision as to whether they should be (a) recommended for implementation, (b) subjected to further investigation, or (c) postponed for later reconsideration;

6. Estimation of the impact on the industrial economy of the activation of the selected development projects, using annual tabulations for a total of five years to make allowance for differing time lags in implementation;

7. Inserting estimates of the effect of new ventures, superimposed on the expected increases of existing industry, into an array of major components of the Gross National Product—such as agriculture, commerce, finance, and the like—to determine whether the growth rate of all industry meets planned objectives.

The use of these techniques should, of course, be a continuing process with progressive refinement of the methodology. At the conclusion of Step 7, fitting the expansion of the industrial component into the growth plan for the Gross National Product, it is highly unlikely that the first round of development opportunities will meet national goals. By feeding additional ideas for new enterprises into the process, the total impact of the industrial component will gradually be increased.

To those who have not used such systematic procedures, this series of steps may appear very formidable, in spite of my assurance that it is practical to apply. To assist in answering such questions, the final section of this chapter is devoted to my personal experience in 1971 in carrying out a comprehensive industrial development survey in Lebanon.

Selection Of Development Opportunities

Preliminary Trial of the Procedures on Accumulated Ideas

It is understandable that the staff of an industrial development project will be loath to wait for results until the methodology described in following sections has been fully worked out. This laudable impatience provides a good excuse to try the procedures on a list of development opportunities which has been collected from previous studies. It can well turn out that among these suggestions several will have such obvious merits that they are felt to be ready for implementation. Furthermore, this exercise will accustom the staff to the methodology, and will give them an opportunity to improve the definition of criteria.

The procedure to be followed is a simplification of the methodology designed for permanent use. The accumulation of prior suggestions is arranged in an array, preferably grouped under the headings of major industrial sectors which have been chosen for regular use. These micro-sectors are then appraised for feasibility by rating them according to their general characteristics, and then, independently, according to their degree of fit to national capabilities; the tests are made by a set of preliminary criteria, which should be refined as a result of additional experience. By inspection of the tabulation, the array of suggestions can be divided into three parts: (a) those that immediately look so good that they can be recommended to entrepreneurs, either private or public, for consideration; (b) those that need more critical examination before firm opinions can be formed; (c) those that appear to be so questionable that they can be tabled for the time being.

The discussion of the most promising opportunities with entrepreneurs will give the interdisciplinary staff a much better conception of the way in which businessmen judge ideas for new ventures. The experience will also indicate the types of public relations activities that need to be evolved for later use. If this dialogue with the world of affairs has the good fortune to result in aggressive action on some proposals, the project will have made an excellent begining.

Compilation of an Array of Industrial Micro-Sectors (Step 1)

The first step in developing the methodology for appraising the feasibility of new ventures is the selection of a list of major sectors of industry (ceramics, chemicals, construction materials, electrical equipment, food products, etc.) and then preparing under each of these headings a list of micro-sectors (for example, under ceramics: bricks, cement blocks, ceramic tile, china dinnerware, etc.). The micro-sectors should include not only those related to present manufactures, but also those of entirely new commodities, which represent, for example, important imports or potential exports.

The selection of the classification system for sectors and micro-sectors should be made very carefully, because it sets the pattern which will be used in the future. When some system is already well entrenched in national statistical data, it should be continued, because in this way it will give the advantage of historical information to show trends, and it will not cause major changes in the usual method for collecting data on the performance of the industrial sector. Where no satisfactory system is being used, or where the present classification is felt to be inadequate, the United Nations has developed an International Standard Industrial Classification of All Economic Activities (UN Sales Number E.68.XVII.8; with a separate detailed index, UN Sales Number 59.XVII.9.) Alternatively, a country might wish to consider adopting the classification of a major trading partner among the highly industrialized nations. It is worthy of mention that in some countries different classifications are used for different functions, for instance in conducting industrial censuses on one hand and in compiling data on imports and exports on the other; where this situation exists some adjustments in the figures must be made to adapt them to the system that is being used for the purpose of investigating new economic opportunities.

The number of micro-sectors listed under each major sector heading should be carefully considered: if there are too few they will not have the desirable technoeconomic homogeneity to make appraisal meaningful; if there are too many, at least in the early stages of applying the procedure, the project staff may feel overwhelmed by the burden of work. As a general guide for practical use, under each major sector heading a list of 10-20 of the most promising micro-sectors might be used at the start, with the expectation of expansion later on. In carrying out diversification studies for industrial clients, my colleagues and I use very fine sub-divisions, in some cases an array of as many as several hundred items.

In the appraisal of industrial opportunities carried out in Lebanon in 1971, I used for screening food processing possibilities a lengthy list,

Selection Of Development Opportunities

for reasons that are especially important in developing countries: they generally have a quite strong base in agricultural raw products and hence utilization of these resources is a logical place to look for industrial opportunities. Underemployment is common in rural areas and any increase in markets or in local pre-processing operations will help to create job opportunities and thus raise the standard of living. There is also much undernourishment in most of these countries and hence any means of conserving food values merits attention. Much wastage of perishable products, even of those that are relatively stable, takes place through mechanical losses, spoilage, and damage by pests; the stimulus of organized utilization programs should help to direct attention toward the reduction of some avoidable wastes of these important renewable resources.

The processes and equipment selected for new ventures in food processing should preferably be as simple, inexpensive, and versatile as possible. The attention of research workers tends to be directed toward exotic processes, such as spray drying, vacuum rollers, freeze drying, and even radiation sterilization, because of their greater professional interest. Such operations may be needed for some specialty products, it is true, but they are expensive to install, involve sophisticated technology, need very careful operating control, and often require large throughputs to attain minimum economic size. On the other hand, there are many possible applications for simpler atmospheric rollers, tray dryers, and sun drying, which are less expensive and more flexible. Versatility is desirable to extend the use of the installations, because short campaigns for perishable produce are one of the troublesome problems of the food processor.

Selection and Definition of Evaluation Criteria (Step 2)

Throughout the procedures described in this chapter, experience has shown that a relatively simple scoring system—H = high, M = medium, L = Low—is satisfactory. More quantitative measures could of course be devised, but those of us who have carried out many studies doubt that these refinements are worth while for making the kinds of comparisons that are involved in screening procedures. When it comes to appraisal of a specific opportunity, however, cost-benefit analysis must be carried out in greater depth.

The list of criteria for the initial screening should be short, preferably only three or four headings each for general characteristics and for degree of fit to local resources. They should be selected on the basis of their primary importance in judging technoeconomic feasibility, which implies interdisciplinary judgment. In Step 4, a somewhat longer list of criteria may be used to obtain more critical appraisal of those candidate micro-sectors which have survived the preliminary screening.

Criteria for General Characteristics (Step 2A)

These facets of industrial potential examine historical trends or informed opinion. In advanced economies there exists considerably more factual background in the form of quantitative data than will be found in developing countries, so that the importance of calling on advisory assistance from outside sources is greater in the latter case. Where there is little internal experience on which to base judgment, greater reliance must be placed on information about other countries which are believed to show a comparable situation.

Growth Rate: When data are available from previous censuses of manufactures, the estimates can be based on them. When facts are lacking, reliance has to be placed on the judgment of individual entrepreneurs, trade association officials and commercial bankers, who have to make such forecasts to consider the justification for loans.

Scoring must be adjusted to reflect the broad movement of the particular economy. As an example, "high" might be used for an anticipated annual rate of growth greater than 10 percent, "medium" for 5-10 percent, and "low" for less than 5 percent.

Profitability: This characteristic is naturally of great importance to entrepreneurs as a means of deciding whether the risks of investment are counterbalanced by the prospects for gain. The greater the degree of innovation, and hence risk, the greater should be the chance of return. Because of high interest rates coupled with inflationary trends, a higher rate of profit is usually required in developing countries.

Data on profitability are by no means easy to obtain. In developed countries, the figures come to light through accounts in business and trade papers, reports of companies, reviews made by banks, and government studies, but even these often require confirmation by further inquiry. In developing countries still greater reliance must be placed on outside sources of information. It is surprising, though, the backlog

Selection Of Development Opportunities

of data that continuing efforts will produce in a reasonable period of time.

In regard to scoring, the degree of innovation must be taken into account. The rate of return on other types of investment must also be considered. In a country with a high interest rate and rapid inflation, for very novel new enterprises "high" may be assigned to ventures with a profitability of 40 percent or more of turnover, "medium" for 20-40 percent, and "low" less than 20 percent. When a reduced degree of innovation and risk is involved, these figures may be reduced, for example, by one-third or one-half.

Investment: The amount of capital required for an installation of minimum economic size, which may vary from country to country unless the installation is subjected to the forces of world competition, is an important subject in developing countries, in which funds for industrial investment are limited. Depending on the local situation, the following scheme might be suitable: "high" is for projects with a capital requirement of more than U.S. $1,000,000, "medium" for U.S. $250,000-1,000,000, and "low" for less than U.S. $250,000.

Availability of Technology: These criteria are chiefly the concern of technologists and engineers who are members of the interdisciplinary teams. The following scoring system is suggested: "high" denotes know-how which already exists or is easily obtained, "medium" for expertise that can be acquired or adapted at reasonable cost, while "low" is for information and skills that do not exist in the country and must be obtained from abroad at considerable expense.

Criteria of Compatibility with Local Resources (Step 2B)

In order to determine how well the individual development opportunity could be handled in the local environment, the same lists of micro-sectors should be examined separately by other appropriate criteria. Again, the number of these test headings should be kept small for screening, with the understanding that a new, more rigorous set may be applied for later critical evaluation. Screening criteria that would be suitable for most developing countries are described in the following discussion.

Raw Materials and Equipment: The scoring system suggested is "high" for projects for which most of the raw materials are indigenous and nearly all the essential equipment and auxiliaries can be obtained within the country, "medium" when this situation is only partly true, and "low" when the major raw materials and equipment components have to be imported.

Human Resources: The essential components are managerial skills for general direction, marketing expertise, manufacturing capabilities, technologic competence, and, to a less extent, an adequate supply of trained or trainable workers; (in most developing countries, it is my experience that there is opportunity to develop operator skills during start-up, the major problem more likely being a high turnover of personnel.) These scores are largely subjective, and if they are greatly in error, they can cause severe problems in conducting the enterprise. A suggested scoring procedure is: "high" when all the skills are believed to be available, "medium" when some are not strong, and "low" when the level of expertise is deficient to the extent that major training efforts will be required.

Capital Requirements: Under Step 2A, information will have been developed regarding the cost of installing a plant of minimum economic size. In this part of the screening process, the significance of "high," "medium," and "low" is obvious as a measure of the ease of obtaining the required funds from local sources.

Conformance with National Goals: These are especially important criteria when the enterprise is expected to need some kind of public support. The major goals in most developing countries are: contribution to health of the economy, creation of employment opportunities, replacement of imports, upgrading of raw materials, or establishment of basic industries which encourage the growth of secondary satellite enterprises. Guidelines from the government are often available in written form, but they may be so general that they require interpretation. The rating scheme depends on composite judgment as to whether the proposed development represents an important contribution to one or more of these objectives, a moderate stimulus, or is not covered by any specific provision.

Screening Procedure for Selecting Favorable Micro-Sectors (Step 3)

From the array of micro-sectors produced by Step 1, the selection of those that appear to be most promising is carried out by applying the criteria described in Step 2. The procedure involves three successive operations: (a) scoring the micro-sectors according to their in-

Table 10
SCREENING PROCEDURE for DEVELOPMENT OPPORTUNITIES
(Scoring system: H—High, M—Medium, L—Low)

General Characteristics				Array of Micro-Sectors		Fit to National Capabilities			
Growth Rate	Profitability	Capital Investment	Availability of Technology	Grouped under Major Sectors	Approval for Evaluation	Raw Materials and Equipment	Human Resources	Capital Requirements	Conformance with National Goals
				Sector I					
				Micro-Sector 1 Micro-Sector 2 Micro-Sector 3 etc.					
				Sector II					
				Micro-Sector 21 Micro-Sector 22 Micro-Sector 23 etc.					
				Sector III					
				Micro-Sector 41 Micro-Sector 42 Micro-Sector 43 etc.					

herent characteristics; (b) rating them independently in regard to their degree of fit to national capabilities; (c) by visual inspection of the two sets of scores, choosing those that appear promising from both points of view. A convenient mechanism is to use a tabulation such as that shown in Table 10.

Array of Micro-Sectors. In the middle part of the table the micro-sectors proposed for evaluation are listed under the headings of major industrial sectors. They are given this position so that they can be referred to most easily for recording the scores on the left side and right side, respectively, by the two sets of criteria. In addition, a separate column is included for a suitable check-mark to denote those micro-sectors which have been chosen for further evaluation as potential candidates for new enterprises.

Criteria of General Characteristics. In the left-hand part of the table, four columns are shown for recording the individual scores for the array of micro-sectors, using the simple system of high, medium, and low. The column headings shown are for growth rate, profitability, capital investment, and availability of technology, as proposed previously. Different criteria may of course be used, but these appear to be of general applicability.

Criteria of Fit to National Capabilities. In the right-hand part of the table, four columns are shown for scoring the micro-sectors in regard to their compatibility with the existing resources of the nation, using the same simple system of rating. The column headings are for raw materials and equipment, human resources, capital requirements, and conformance with national goals, which appear to be the most critical factors in determining the feasibility of new ventures from the local point of view. Other criteria may of course be substituted or added.

In making these evaluations it is desirable that they be free from any influence that might be exerted by knowledge of the ratings for general characteristics. This may be easily accomplished by placing a temporary mask over the left-hand part of the tabulation.

Selection of Promising Micro-sectors by Inspection. The final procedure is to run down all three parts of the table to choose those micro-sectors which are judged to have attractive potential. Those which have high scores for both general characteristics and fit to resources of

Selection Of Development Opportunities 151

the country are obvious selections. On the other hand, a micro-sector which is rated as having a low growth rate and low profitability may show such excellent fit to local capabilities or national policy that it is worth including in the preferred list. Hence the selection process should be carried out with broad perspective instead of rigid ground rules. The value of the system lies in the fact that it induces logical comparison of the merits of a range of micro-sectors competing for development efforts.

Critical Appraisal of Selected Micro-Sectors (Step 4)

Those micro-sectors that pass the screening test are then subjected to more rigorous examination in order to prepare a revised list which the evaluation team believes to be ready for decision as to course of action.

The criteria to be used in this step offer a wide range of choices. The previous headings may be used with more rigorous analysis. The scoring system may be amplified by enlarging the number of grades, for example, to excellent, high, good, medium, and low. Redefined criteria may be substituted for some or all of those used previously; examples are given below to illustrate the range of options available.

The examination of inherent characteristics may be expanded by substituting "domestic market potential" and "export market potential" for "growth rate." "Value added" is a factor emphasized in some countries. "Industrial profile" is sometimes considered important to distinguish between markets dominated by one or a few large enterprises, as in primary raw materials, and those characterized by open competition among a number of small firms. The question of "franchise" may arise to distinguish between those micro-sectors in which a new entrant has to face entrenched brand names or high customer preference and those in which there are no barriers of this type.

The citeria of fit to national capability may also be expanded by inserting new ones such as "raw materials," "utilities requirements," and "availability of technology," although these were included in the more general subject headings listed earlier. Where the proposed micro-sector is closely related to existing operations, "utilization of installed capacity" may indicate that it would be better to tie it to an established firm. "Strategic impact" is a special aspect of conformance to national goals, and may be broken down into foreign exchange generation, replacement of imports, upgrading of raw materials, or some similar classification.

Decision on Course of Action (Step 5)

The shortened list of attractive micro-sectors is now at the critical stage of decision. At this point the advisory opinions of entrepreneurs are especially valuable. The courses of action in individual cases may be: (a) speedy promotion of very promising opportunities; (b) further investigation of some aspects; (c) institution of a development project; (d) postponement or abandonment in spite of earlier favorable opinions.

When the concept appears to qualify in all respects, promotional mechanisms should be considered. If it is merely included in a list recommended by the government, the chance of its being grasped by an entrepreneur is much reduced. Instead, an orderly search should be made in the industrial community to find an interested executive, and then any additional information should be sought to answer his questions about commercial feasibility.

In other cases the project may seem to be very attractive, but there is need for additional confirmation of one or more aspects, such as size of market or availability of raw materials or equipment. When the questions have been cleared up, the opportunity is ready for promotion.

In still other instances the gap in information may be so large as to call for a special investigation. For example, technical confirmation of process feasibility may be needed, or market research to study customer reaction in considerable depth.

Finally, in spite of all earlier favorable opinions, some ideas will fail to survive the moment of truth. Rather than beating them to death in desperate attempts to keep them alive, it is better to table them, at least for the present, and turn attention to more likely candidates.

Estimation of Total Impact of New Industrial Ventures (Step 6)

To complete the story of the benefits of industrial development, a composite summary of expectations for all recommended undertakings should be compiled. A convenient form for this step is shown in Table 11, regarding which a number of comments are given below.

The summary is best organized in terms of major sectors of industry, because it is principally for the use of senior executives in government who generally will not be interested in all the details. To obtain

Table 11
ESTIMATED IMPACT OF NEW VENTURES ON THE INDUSTRIAL ECONOMY
(In constant monetary units, base year 19   )

Summation of Projects in Micro-Sectors under Major Sectors	19			19			19			19			19		
	Existing Industry	New Ventures	Total	Existing Industry	New Ventures	Total	Existing Industry	New Ventures	Total	Existing Industry	New Ventures	Total	Existing Industry	New Ventures	Total
Sector I															
Sector II															
Sector III															
Sector IV															
Sector V															
etc.															

the data for this purpose, however, a very large amount of back-up information on individual micro-sectors must be carried out.

In nearly all countries there is today an underlying growth of existing industry, although of course some of the component manufactures may be showing a decline. Appraisal of the effect of the industrial development program should therefore superimpose the projected benefits from new ventures on the trends for established lines of activity. The table illustrates a simple manner of doing this.

The true situation will be masked by inflation; where the rate is high, the distortion is particularly misleading. The use of monetary units of constant value, using a fixed base period, is therefore highly desirable.

The table is designed to show the money value of industrial production. Its form can obviously be modified to an appraisal of changes in gainful employment, in the deployment of capital resources, or other significant economic factors.

Combination of Industrial Growth with other Major Economic Elements (Step 7)

For broad national planning, the projected gains from industrial growth should be consolidated with other major elements of the economy, such as agriculture, construction, and financial operations. The existing system of national accounts provides the classification, and the data for other major elements should be compiled in similar fashion. A suitable form of presentation is embodied in Table 12. Here too it is desirable to use monetary units of constant value to eliminate the effects of inflation.

Rarely indeed will the first round of proposed new manufacturing undertakings satisfy either the national planners or the industrial development staff. Hence a return to Step 1 will be needed to enlarge the list of micro-sectors for appraisal. This longer array can be carried forward, not only for scoring the added items, but also for re-evaluating those in the original list.

Dynamic industrial development programs should be continuing processes, with progressive enlargement of the number of opportunities and refinement of the criteria.

Table 12
Incorporation of Projected Industrial Growth Into The National Master Plan
(In constant monetary units, base year 19____)

Major Elements of the Economy	19____	19____	19____	19____	19____
A. Agriculture					
B. _____					
C. _____					
D. _____					
E. _____					
G. _____					
F. Industry					
H. _____					
etc.					

General Comments on the Procedures

The chain of steps outlined in preceding sections is a process of synthesis, that is, building up from estimates for individual micro-sectors. This procedure of funneling detailed findings into the formulation of a general plan is greatly superior, in my opinion, to setting arbitrary goals a priori. The latter method is in essence forcing the conclusions regarding individual undertakings into a preconceived framework. The synthetic approach gives a more realistic foundation for planning.

In regard to the conventional use of a five-year plan, I much prefer a rolling projection for successive five-year periods. This applies particularly to such summaries as those shown in Table 11 and Table 12, and of course to the detailed studies on which they are based. Rolling estimates have two major advantages: (a) they encourage periodic adjustment of goals to conform to current experience, instead of delaying corrections to the end; (b) they relieve the planners of the stigma of final large deficits in performance by providing these interim modifications to reflect reality.

Methodology in an Industrial Development Study in Lebanon

In this section I will describe a study conducted in Lebanon during September-November 1971 to propose strategy for an industrial development program. This example is cited to demonstrate the practicality of the methodology previously presented.

Having been appointed as UNDP/UNIDO Senior Consultant on Industrial Development for this project, I spent the first two weeks in developing contacts and planning my three-month program. I enjoyed complete freedom in carrying out the study according to my own ideas, with only information reports to the United Nations officials responsible for the project, who were also extremely helpful in briefing me on the local situation, with which I was generally familiar as a result of several previous visits. I was able to complete my assignment in this short time because of freedom from interference and because of previous experience in similar studies elsewhere. I was given part-time staff assistance by the Lebanese agencies which were most interested, and this help was very useful in selecting interviewees and arranging appointments, as well as in informal checking of findings and conclusions.

Selection Of Development Opportunities 157

The interdisciplinary nature of this preliminary survey should be stressed. Time did not permit the use of desirable series of teams to cover the range of industrial sectors, but my findings and conclusions were reviewed informally with local experts. Their helpful comments were reflected in my report, but I take full responsibility for interpretations and conclusions.

I first scanned reports of earlier studies to glean any information that would be helpful. In this connection, it is a sad fact that in many countries there are large files of successive studies which have not resulted in any appreciable action. To save time I wrote separate memoranda on individual phases as they were completed; 11 of these were included as appendices to my report, amounting to almost as many words as the body of the report. I visited 31 industrial plants, and had contacts with representatives of five Ministries, a dozen local professional and industrial organizations, five financial institutions, nine university departments, and commercial attachés of four foreign embassies. I had many contacts with personnel in several UN agencies. In addition I wrote and delivered a three-part series of lectures on "The Management of Development Projects" at the American University of Beirut, and presented two talks on cost-benefit relationships in export stimulation and on productivity in industry at UN international conferences; copies were distributed to the participants and to a considerable number of public officials and industrial executives.

The mission in Lebanon ended on November 30 with submission of my final report. This included a brief summary; an overview of Lebanese industry and its capabilities; an outline of methodology for screening and evaluating individual micro-sectors of industry; a list of approximately 60 suggestions for new types of products or expansion of existing manufactures, with initial proposals for government activities to stimulate development; a review of the status of major sectors of industry; more detailed discussion of helpful government programs; and a proposal for UNDP/UNIDO technical assistance over a five-year period.

This situation with respect to continuation of the Lebanese project points up a severe weakness in many consulting engagements, for both private clients and public agencies, in that they do not take advantage of the consultant's objective appraisal of the clients' organization and its operations in an advisory capacity during implementation. I have seen all too many cases in which recommendations enthusiastically accepted by clients' executives were woefully mauled in execution as a result of internal pressures or lack of objectivity. Failure to make additional use of this expertise of consultants often has a financial aspect, in that the cost of in-house staff groups is borne as a routine expense, often without adequate knowledge of the full cost when true overheads are applied, and without critical review of cost-benefit aspects of their programs; consultants' fees, on the other hand, represent new money outside regular budgets, and require special authorization.

Other weaknesses in projects for international development agencies are that they rarely provide for an exploratory trip by the consultant to get a first-hand view of the situation; and generally his views are not adequately reflected in the definition of the mission, because these are usually negotiated beforehand between sponsoring agency and the host government. The cost of a preliminary short round-trip visit would be more than paid for by better definition of project scope, more constructive briefing, and a faster start on the program after arrival.

If the Lebanese study had been extended to a second phase, the first month would have been spent in discussions with government officials and other good sources of opinion, and in organizing the project staff. Adequate staffing for the action phase would have consisted of three economists; one expert each in market research, process engineering, and public relations; three secretaries; and two chauffeured automobiles.

After this introductory period, the course of work during the next six months would have taken the following chief directions: improvement in the criteria and methodology for appraising development opportunities, particularly to train the counterpart staff; organization of four small advisory groups representing respectively government planning agencies, industrial management, technology and engineering, and development finance; expansion of the list of candidate microsectors and more critical analysis of their merits; formulation of a government program to stimulate industrial growth; design and execution of public relations activities to arouse entrepreneurial interest; consultation with public and quasi-public agencies and institutions on means of improving their services to industry; initial organization of

Selection Of Development Opportunities

discussion groups to improve practices in technical management and the technoeconomic disciplines of market research and engineering evaluation of projects.

At the end of the six-month period the program should have been well developed and in condition to be turned over to a government agency for administration.

CHAPTER TWELVE

IMPLEMENTATION OF DEVELOPMENT OPPORTUNITIES

In Chapter Ten, promotional activities of the government to stimulate new enterprises were listed. In the present discussion, these will be amplified. The responsibilities of private entrepreneurs will be defined in general terms. A procedure for applying both types of activities to specific cases will be proposed. This methodology was used by the author to check his conclusions in the Lebanese study described at the end of Chapter Eleven.

Government Activities to Assist Implementation

Public activities for aiding new industrial enterprises are of two types: First, certain general programs provide the infrastructure to assist entrepreneurs in making their decisions, and these will be discussed in the earlier paragraphs. Secondly, certain cases require special assistance; instances will be pointed out in the following material.

In nearly all countries, the establishment of new ventures is subject to control by some form of licensing. In the use of these licensing powers, and in decisions as to any government assistance, public officials should choose a middle ground to encourage orderly economic development. If enforcement is too strict, the initiative of entrepreneurs will be discouraged. If policies are too lax, particularly in developing countries, national resources may be dissipated on unsuccessful undertakings. The situation calls for sympathetic, mutual understanding of the respective problems on the part of both government officials and entrepreneurs, whether they be in the private or public sector.

Policy and Program for Industrial Development. If public officials and potential investors have to consider each opportunity as an entirely new case, not governed by a general policy, they both will waste their time exploring in each instance all details of what the government may be prepared to do to assist them. This leads to haphazard and inconsistent decisions which further complicate the situation by requiring rationalization as to why the measures adopted in one example do not apply also to others. If, instead, the framework of a rational program is developed as a basis for analyzing particulars, the whole process can be carried out in an atmosphere of orderly thinking.

Development Financing. Because of the difficulties in many developing countries of obtaining the capital for new ventures, the government should pay particular attention to the mechanisms by which funds are provided for industrial expansion. The operation of development banks, which are usually quasi-public institutions with considerable autonomy, should be analyzed to determine how they can best promote growth opportunities. Commercial banks in developing countries usually concentrate on short-range loans for supporting the needs of trading operations; means of enlisting their interest in longer-term industrial loans should be considered. The nature of capital formation within the country—including reinvested earnings, public savings, and government resources—should be studied with a view to trying to increase the funds available for entrepreneurial undertakings in accordance with national growth plans.

Market Information. The government should devote attention to the possibility of increasing the quantity and quality of marketing data, on which decisions regarding new undertakings must be made. In most developing countries, the volume of information is much too scanty. For export marketing, the situation is even worse; the activities of commercial attachés in leading trading partners should be broadened to provide intelligence on size of market, quality specifications, trade practices, and character of competition. Trade agreements are often a useful tool for increasing the volume of products moving abroad.

Importation of Raw Materials and Equipment. Industrial development is often hampered by restrictions on obtaining materials and essential items of equipment. The system of imposing import duties and the paper work required for licenses should be carefully reviewed to remove undesirable obstacles.

Encouragement of Foreign Technology, Know-How, and Capital. When the need for means of increasing resources for industrial development is recognized, all regulations respecting importation of skills and for securing financial participation should be reviewed to provide an attractive climate for the inflow of those components which are considered to be in the national interest.

Implementation Of Projects 163

Development of Institutions to Aid Enterpreneurs. Public support is usually needed to stimulate the development of agencies and insitutions to supply the skills needed to support industrial development. Some may be provided by government departments, but many are in the domain of autonomous quasi-public organizations or private consultancies. Competence in technoeconomic evaluations, market research techniques, information and technical services, and managerial practices are particularly important. Training opportunities for factory operators to develop their skills are a matter of national concern.

Pre-investment Prospectuses. Many opportunities will closely resemble types of manufactures already being carried on in the country; the potential benefits and risks will therefore be quite apparent to entrepreneurs. For more innovative undertakings, however, to attract the attention of the investment community, more positive measures should be taken, and pre-investment prospectuses are one of the most effective devices. They present information about promising opportunities in the form which is most readily understood by entrepreneurs.

Development Subsidies. This is a major consideration in many cases. Financial support may be required for certain fledgling enterprises to put them on a self-sustaining basis, or it may be desirable to maintain selected industries judged to be of importance to the national well-being. The difficulty is, of course, that every entrepreneur would welcome a subsidy. Each favorable decision creates a precedent, and reasons for turning down a related request can be the source of much controversy. Each case, therefore, requires very careful consideration to try to differentiate between self-interest and the country's welfare. Some subsidies may be granted for sharing the cost of start-up or for encouraging export trade.

Protection Against Imports. Protective tariffs are the most obvious form of nurturing a new venture, but there are other safeguards against imports which impede the development of local industry. Anti-dumping regulations are often rather superficial and difficult to enforce; they often do not peer behind the scenes for hidden subsidies. Inspection of quality of imported goods helps to insure fair competition with local manufactures.

Evaluation of Social Benefits. The contributions of a new enterprise to the national social goals are very difficult to appraise because there are no adequate yardsticks to measure them. Decisions are, therefore, likely to be based on personal opinions. There are all too many examples in developing countries of poorly located plants, the sites for which were selected to provide employment in depressed regions, with the result that they are far removed from the sources of bulky raw materials and from their markets. Eventually many are closed down because of high costs; those that remain operating are a net drag on the economy. The best answer is thorough investigation of alternative courses of action to select those types of economic activity which best fit the composite requirements of the region and the nation without disproportionate harm to the economy.

Responsibilities of Entrepreneurs

While the government can do much to provide assistance to entrepreneurs, the onus rests on the latter to make careful investigation of the factors which will safeguard their investments. Here, too, the requirements comprise both generally applicable procedures and those which are influenced by the particular nature of the venture.

Technoeconomic Feasibility Studies. In spite of the availability of pertinent statistical data supplied from public sources, and in spite of the quality of pre-investment prospectuses which may have been prepared at the instigation of the government, the entrepreneur is negligent who does not provide himself with a competent feasibility study of his proposed venture. He may carry out the study himself, engage a consultant, or use the services of some agency which the government has assisted to acquire the necessary skills. The investigation must include a detailed cost-benefit appraisal of the precise dimensions of the enterprise as he intends to carry it out.

Market Confirmation. The size, composition, trade practices, and competitive situation of the marketplace should be included in technoeconomic feasibility study. However, the marketing prospects are so vitally important to the success of a venture that the subject is re-emphasized here by a separate heading. The confirmation may need to be carried as far as a test marketing program, using representative samples of the commodities which are to be offered.

Development of Skills. The entrepreneur must assess, as an important aspect of an innovative project, the range of skills which his organization must possess or acquire. If it is necessary to develop expertise, there are several routes by which this can be done. He may hire one or more experts on a temporary or permanent basis.

He may arrange for the training of his personnel by training trips abroad, taking advantage of fellowships offered by his government or an international agency. He may engage a consultant. He may use a visiting expert to provide on-the-job training for his employees; the U.S. International Executive Service Corps, for example, provides experts, often retired industrialists, who serve without salary but with their living costs paid by the client, and similar arrangements are offered by other industrialized countries.

Protection of New Enterprises. The venture may require some form of protection—such as protective tariffs or anti-dumping regulations—to insure viability. The entrepreneur should check carefully with public officials the kinds of safeguards he may reasonably expect and any prospective changes in these provisions.

Participation of Foreign Interests. The proposed venture may, in the opinion of its sponsors, depend heavily on foreign technology, managerial skills, or capital. The entrepreneurs should clarify with government agencies the conditions that govern the obtaining of this external assistance.

Utilities: Some micro-sectors are dependent on economical sources of utilities, particularly electric power. Because the operations of most public utility enterprises are directly or indirectly influenced by government policies, entrepreneurs should determine with the appropriate officials the most favorable rates they can negotiate.

Requirements for Government Promotion and Enterpreneurial Action

The micro-sectors of industry recommended for implementation, as a result of the appraisal in Step 5 of Chapter Eleven, are now ready for decision on what else needs to be done to move them forward toward commercialization. There are two major aspects: (1) government promotional activities and (2) steps to be taken by the entrepreneurs themselves. The methodology for this purpose is summarized in Chart V. The need for special attention in the individual micro-sectors is shown by inserting checks in the appropriate columns.

The tabulation consists of four main sections: (1) a listing below the title of those government and entrepreneurial activities which have a common requirement for all proposed ventures; (2) a middle section showing the recommended micro-sectors, including a sub-section for indicating the nature of the impact on the industrial complex of the country; (3) a left-hand section for checking the special government activity needed for any individual undertaking; (4) a right-hand section to show the particular requirements that should be considered by entrepreneurs before a firm decision is reached to proceed with implementation.

Promotional Activities of Government. To repeat a conclusion expressed earlier, if a government limits its activities to passive expression of interest in the growth of the industrial sector, even though it defines the types of manufactures which it believes to be most suitable for the country, there is a good probability that not much will happen, unless the entrepreneurial spirit is very strong. If, on the other hand, the administration adopts an aggressive posture toward industrialization, it will undertake a promotional program to stimulate the interest of the business community. The nature of these activities is discussed in the following presentation.

Government Activities Applicable to All Micro-Sectors. Several types of programs that are needed for all new industrial ventures are listed above the body of the table. Because they have this general applicability, public planning agencies should devote careful analysis to the adequacy of existing and proposed activities to carry them out.

Policy and Program for Stimulating Industrial Development. The subjects that are suitable for coverage in these public declarations of the intentions of government have already been described in Chapter Ten. The views of advisory groups of industrialists and financiers should be sought to make them as forceful, complete, and workable as possible. They provide the basic documents on which the other activities are built. They should be reviewed periodically to improve and clarify their wording.

Development Financing. The availability of funds for financing new ventures is a very important aspect of industrial development. The operation of public or quasi-public loan agencies such as development banks should be analyzed. A favorable climate should be created to encourage commercial banks to participate in the activity. Systems of soft government loans or guarantees of funding by other institutions may be used.

Market Information. Data on consumption patterns, an important public function which has long been used in mature economies, is being provided to increasing extent in developing countries, but still

CHART V

REQUIREMENTS FOR GOVERNMENT PROMOTION AND ENTREPRENEURIAL ACTION

Government Activities Applicable to All Micro-Sectors:

(1) Policy and program for industrial development, (2) Development financing, (3) Market information, (4) Importation of raw materials and equipment, (5) Encouragement for foreign technology and capital, (6) Strengthening institutions providing development services

Entrepreneurial Activities Needed for All Micro-Sectors:

(1) Techno-economic feasibility studies, (2) Market confirmation

GOVERNMENT PROMOTION					ARRAY OF RECOMMENDED MICRO-SECTORS OF INDUSTRY GROUPED UNDER MAJOR SECTORS	INDUSTRIAL IMPACT			ENTREPRENEURIAL ACTIVITIES				
Pre-Investment Prospectus	Development Subsidy for Start-up or Long-term	Protection Against Imports	Policy Regarding Utilities	Appraisal of Social Benefits		New Industry	Expansion of Existing Industry	Time Required for Implementation in Years	Development of Skills	Protection for Start-up or Long-term	Foreign Technology and Know-how	Foreign Capital	Special Requirements for Utilities
					Sector I Micro-Sector 1 Micro-Sector 2 Micro-Sector 3 etc. Sector II Micro-Sector 21 Micro-Sector 22 etc. Sector III Micro-Sector 41 etc.								

needs much expansion. The wealthy countries have sufficient economic resilience to absorb the losses due to failed businesses, which usually occur because of lack of managerial competence or an insufficient back-log of working capital to tide them over the start-up period. In developing nations, however, the consequences of unsuccessful ventures are not only a set-back to the economy, but also a deterrent to entrepreneurial morale. Hence, the provision of data regarding the size and character of markets, on which backers of new enterprises can rely for better forecasts of sales potential, is an important responsibility of government.

Availability of Imported Raw Materials and Equipment. It is not uncommon to find two different government departments working at cross-purposes in regard to the conditions for importing raw materials and essential items of equipment. On the one hand, the development agency is striving to promote and nurture new industrial ventures. On the other, the officials who have responsibility for controlling foreign trade may be locked into an antiquated schedule of regulations on imports and exports designed to produce revenue; they are slow to change their practices for the different objective of stimulating industrial development.

Foreign Technology and Capital. In this case, too, different philosophies may result in impasses. A nationalistic policy to encourage internal self-reliance and independence from foreign influence may place severe barriers in the way of obtaining needed components for new undertakings. Some compromise between the two points of view must be reached to enable certain selected types of operations to attain a healthy basis for establishment and growth.

Up-grading Sources of Service to Industry. The major types of organizations which need encouragement and public support to perfect their skills are those providing information and technical services, technoeconomic capabilities, including market research, management development, and the training of workers. These may be in the public, quasi-public or private sectors.

Special Types of Government Assistance in Certain Micro-Sectors. On the left-hand side of the tabulation, five columns are provided for checking the need for various types of special assistance from the government under the headings: (1) Pre-Investment Prospectus, (2) Development Subsidy for Start-up or Long-term, (3) Protection

Against Imports, (4) Policy Regarding Utilities, (5) Appraisal of Social Benefits. Although these should be largely self-explanatory, brief descriptions are given in the following paragraphs. The number of check marks in each column will give government officials a rough measure of the relative importance of the services in the total economy.

Pre-Investment Prospectus. Summaries of cost-benefit relationships and advantages are most important for micro-sectors that are entirely new to the country, because entrepreneurs cannot base their interest on the demonstrated success of related types of business.

Development Subsidy for Start-up or Long-term. It has been pointed out earlier that practically all investors would like to have the advantage of some form of subsidy. Because there are limits to the number and size of such concessions which the government has the resources to grant, careful analysis must be carried out to determine those cases in which public support is essential.

Protection Against Imports. The situation here is similar to that for subsidies, because nearly all entrepreneurs would like to have preferred status. All forms of protection have the effect of increasing the internal prices of the commodities; hence, discriminating judgment must be used to strike an equitable balance.

Policy Regarding Utilities. Because most installations for public utilities are under government regulation, those micro-sectors of industry which are particularly vulnerable to high costs for these elements of expense may need price concessions to become viable.

Appraisal of Social Benefits. In the case of micro-sectors that rely for approval on claims of contributions to social welfare, best efforts must be put forth by public planners to decide whether economic disadvantages are counterbalanced by the social gain.

Responsibilities of Entrepreneurs for Determining Feasibility of Undertakings

As in the case of government promotional activities, the steps that entrepreneurs should take fall into two categories, namely: (1) those that apply to all proposals and (2) those that relate to the specific requirements of a given micro-sector.

Entrepreneurial Activities Needed for All Micro-Sectors. The necessity for basing decisions on rigorous technoeconomic feasibility analyses and market investigations is self-evident. It is worth mentioning,

Implementation Of Projects

however, that in some cases, when the venture is to receive the benefit of a development loan, the cost of these studies may, for approved applications, be included in the corpus of the loans.

Development of Skills. The entrepreneur should carefully consider the range of skills necessary for the conduct of his venture and the best way to supplement those that are deficient, including the possibility of securing financial support for the training programs.

Protection. The proposer of a new enterprise should determine through public officials the nature of protection measures which he can expect.

Foreign Technology. Here too, it is the responsibility of the entrepreneur to investigate the conditions governing his reliance on technical help or licenses from abroad.

Foreign Capital. The same situation as in the preceding section applies here also.

Requirements for Utilities. The technoeconomic evaluation will reveal the relevance of the cost of utilities to the success of the venture. When this expense is a determining factor, the entrepreneur will need to explore the possibility of negotiating more favorable rates.

Comprehensive Review Before Final Decision. The urgent need for a final critical review of all facets of a proposed venture has been emphasized in Chapter Four. This requirement is imperative in developing countries to protect resources and entrepreneurial drive.

The comprehensive appraisal should cover the requirements of managerial skills, technologic base, manufacturing competence, marketing know-how, compliance with regulations and national interest, and financial resources. If the organization is seriously deficient in any respect, the success of the undertaking is in jeopardy.

Conclusion

Discussions of industrial development in underdeveloped countries all too frequently emphasize only the need for technology transfer from advanced economies. This is an unfortunate oversimplification, because growth in the manufacturing sector is even more dependent on the acquisition of managerial skills to use the technology effectively, and these skills are very subject to cultural differences.

Governments are responsible for creating a favorable climate to encourage new ventures. The entrepreneurs themselves must take advantage of opportunities to improve their managerial and technologic expertise in order to establish new enterprises which will justify the investment and at the same time contribute to the national welfare.

The creation of an environment conducive to growth of the manufacturing sector is primarily the responsibility of the government. This industrial infra-structure, preferably assigned to a specific ministry or agency, should set forth the policies and orderly programs for directions and amount of expansion called for in national planning. It should be based on analysis of the country's human and physical resources. It should involve objective review of all government activities that affect the attractiveness of new ventures.

The individual entrepreneurs in both private and public sectors must select the specific opportunities to which they can devote their efforts and capital with a satisfactory degree of assurance. They must examine critically the requirements for successful operation and build up the resources of their organizations for this purpose. The development of a broad spectrum of managerial capabilities is vital for the transfer of new commercial systems to developing countries.

The nation can look forward to healthy sustained growth only if the government infra-structure for development and the enlightened entrepreneurship of industrialists are in harmony.

APPENDIX
HOW TO START TASK FORCE SYSTEMS

The recommendations in this appendix are based on personal experience in assisting clients in a wide variety of organizations to install interdisciplinary systems. While they are presented here chiefly in relation to new product development, as one of the simplest cases to explain, the same procedures are suitable for use in the many other applications mentioned in earlier chapters.

The change from the formal channels of a rigidly structured organization to the open and informal relationships of task forces is a traumatic experience for many participants unless the shift is made gradually. If the transition is abrupt, the result will be chaos. The slower but surer course of experimental introduction should be undertaken as an educational process to show the staff how the system works; a few cases should be used as training examples.

The internal climate of the organization needed for the smooth functioning of task forces has been described in Chapter Six. Here the emphasis will be on the specific steps to be taken in introducing them.

A primary factor in success is the attitude of the managers at top and middle levels. They must share the conviction that the procedure is a good idea. They must make sure that the test cases are given a fair trial. They must make it clear to the staff that they give wholehearted support to the concept. Any who will not accept these requirements should be by-passed in setting up the initial demonstrations.

The behavior of these managers must conform with their good intentions. If some members of the groups which they administer become members of teams, they must refrain from any actions which infringe on the complete freedom of the participants to carry out their roles as independent specialists. If they themselves serve on task forces, they must scrupulously avoid any use of their rank to give weight to their opinions; they must accept with good grace the contrary opinions of their juniors in the administrative hierarchy. If they are on the sidelines, they must not do any meddling which weakens the authority of the team leader or the responsibilities of individual members.

Typical Questions about the Feasibility of Task Forces

In helping organizations adopt interdisciplinary systems, I have heard again and again the same questions and objections. Because they illustrate hurdles to be overcome, some of the most frequent are mentioned here. While there may be a modicum of truth in some of them in certain circumstances, in general they reflect the traditions of the academic communities in which our specialists are trained.

The Impossibility of Programming Research. "You simply can't schedule research and development because the results are unpredictable! That is the very nature of scientific investigations." So say those who have never tried to plan an applied research program, and, what's worse, will never attempt to unless pressure is brought to bear.

There is certainly some truth in the belief that one cannot lay out and follow narrowly a plan for fundamental research. Nevertheless, it is my conviction that many productive scientists of high standing approach a problem the way they would a game of chess. They have a clear grasp of their goals. They plan their moves ahead, so that if such-and-such happens, the next thing to try is this-and-that. They do not wander haphazardly from a single isolated finding to the next, but they are quick to grasp an unexpected result and incorporate it in the next round of planning. Scheduling is possible even in the arts: Verdi composed Aïda under contract to deliver the finished work by a fixed date, and Sir Walter Scott wrote the Waverley Novels on a regular schedule.

If research cannot be programmed, by what strange miracle does it happen that most post-graduate students are able to complete their thesis problems on schedule to get their diplomas with their contemporaries?

The facts of life are that in most well-managed organizations, particularly in industry, the projects are planned and budgeted, except for long-range exploratory investigations. Consulting firms have had to do this as regular practice because their engagements are usually defined by agreements covering date of completion and cost; if the budgets are exceeded, the extra expense is a penalty to be absorbed by the consultant. Cost-plus contracts are rare.

The best answer to this objection about scheduling technical programs is trial-and-error. Some of the initial attempts may be far out

Starting Task Force Systems 175

of line. With practice it becomes second nature for team leaders to plan a program and forecast the effort and expense needed to carry it out.

What Does a Supervisor Find to Do? Naive managers raise the question: "When a manager finds that all members of his group are working on projects supervised by team leaders, what does he have left to do?" This is the least sensible objection. The supervisor, instead of reviewing the activities of his staff and sitting in lengthy planning meetings, has many options which permit him to use his skills in challenging ways: (1) As a manager he has a new level of responsibility for seeing that his group is constructively deployed. (2) He has the same duties of organizational housekeeping to assist his staff in adjusting to their role in the organization. (3) As an active participant in project work, he can spend much more time in the use of his personal expertise, either as a team leader or as a member of other teams; this experience also aids him to better understanding of the problems of professional development faced by others in his group.

The Nuisance of Recording Time Distribution. Unsystematic individuals resist the idea of keeping track of their time. They vocalize their complaint in a round-about way: "Time cards are a bureaucratic nuisance and are not in keeping with professional dignity. I get my best ideas while I am mowing the lawn — how in the world can I put that on a time card!"

The time card system must be rigorously differentiated from a routine attendance record, which is not in general use for professional personnel. For the purpose of task force control, some orderly form of recording the distribution of effort is essential, although it cannot purport to be a measure of creativity, for which we now have no yardstick. It has the advantage of letting the individual see for himself how efficiently he is using his time in order that he may become a better manager of his skills. To regard it as "unprofessional" is rationalization contrary to the fact that many members of the medical and legal professions set fees for their services which approximate their expenditure of effort.

To summarize the discussion of budgetary control of task forces in Chapter Five, supervisors and team leaders must give convincing evidence of the fact that they are using the data as a managerial tool and not as an instrument of bureaucratic procedure. The system must be managed with flexibility to allow for uncertainties in the rate of progress in investigational work. Forecasts of time allocations should be reviewed with reasonable frequency so that they can be revised in the light of actual experience. Time spent on minor assignments and particularly on overhead activities should be accounted for in the least cumbersome manner so that the individual can guard against undue dissipation of his talents in non-project work.

Confusion About Channels of Authority. This is certainly an understandable question, and one that is answered only by experience in a task force system. "Do you mean to say that my direct responsibility in a team is to the team leader and not to my supervisor? And that I am not to check regularly with my boss about the details of what I am doing? After all, he is my boss and he is the one who decides when I get a boost in salary or rank."

The feasibility of operating two parallel systems of administrative control has been discussed in Chapter Six. One is the formal chain of command for setting the role of the individual in relationship to the rest of the organization. The second is for management of professional activities in the framework of projects and task forces. That the two schemes are compatible is proved by their use in many private enterprises and public agencies.

This type of question is seldom asked by self-confident staff members; instead, they thrive on the opportunity to stand on their own professional capabilities without continual surveillance by a superior. But less secure individuals need to feel that the boss is always there to help and advise.

In a smoothly operating system each team member is free to turn to anyone in the organization to get specialized knowledge or counsel. In exercising this privilege, however, he should observe two precautions: First, he should not incur so much effort on the part of a contact that a question of time charges to the project is raised, without prior approval of the team leader. Secondly, because confidential treatment of information may be involved, no disclosures should be made which have security aspects, without proper caution as to its proprietary nature.

A revealing sidelight on the challenge of task force systems is the observation that many senior men prefer the opportunity to make full

Starting Task Force Systems

use of their professional talents rather than dilute them with purely administrative duties.

Prerequisites for Task Force Operations

At the risk of some repetition, this section will be given over to a summary of the conditions necessary for successful use of an interdisciplinary system. The comments apply particularly to the situation that should exist during the start-up period.

Internal Environment. The management hierarchy, or at least those concerned with the demonstration case, must be convinced that a task force operation may be a very beneficial innovation in the use of specialized manpower. It must use care in selecting an area in which favorable results are most likely to occur; in my experience research and development is a good choice. The engineering department may be considered, but it is probably already carrying out its work this way, and in any case everyone expects engineers to follow systematic methods in organizing and conducting their projects.

No matter which department is chosen, not only must its managers and staff be favorable to the demonstration, but also other departments or groups which will be asked to lend some of their specialists on part-time basis must be willing to cooperate. If the individuals in the host department use time cards, which indeed they should, this procedure need not be extended to borrowed personnel from elsewhere in the organization; usually it is better to omit this control technique for outsiders, because the task force idea plus time cards doubles the complications of dealing with them. It is much simpler, for instance, merely to borrow a market researcher from the sales department for ten percent of his time for three months than to raise the issue of time distribution.

Delegation of Responsibility and Authority. The team leader must be given the necessary freedom to select his team members, organize their activities, and control their programs. The team members must enjoy latitude in their release from other duties and their prerogative to operate without hindrance in cooperation with the team leader. Any infraction of these requirements is harmful to the validity of the trial.

Practical Demonstration of Task Force Methodology

This concluding section will be devoted to the mechanics of carrying out the operation of a task force for the purpose of demonstrating the feasibility and advantages of the procedure. I recommend that at most only one or two test cases be used at the start. To try to do more will tend to confuse an organization which has not used the system before. After a successful demonstration has been completed, say, in a period of three or four months, the methodology can be gradually extended to other projects.

Selection of Functional Area. Care should be exercised in the choice of the department in which the demonstration is to be carried out. It is essential that the managers and staff be receptive to the idea. The type of activity should be one in which the merits of a broader approach are clearly visible. To this end, it is highly desirable that the results of the completed study be in such form that the status of the project can be compared with what it might have been by the cellular procedures used previously.

My first choice is the research and development department when this is a separate function in the organization. In this opinion I am doubtless influenced by the fact that it is the area in which I have had longest experience in interdisciplinology, both in actual practice and in guiding clients in the introduction of the procedures. On the other hand, the end result has the great advantage of being in tangible form, instead of a report with recommendations, as a new product which one can see and feel.

The decision regarding the other disciplines to be included in the team resources is also quite obvious for new product development. The object is to define an end item which can be made by an industrially feasible process to meet demonstrable market acceptance. If this is left entirely to the technologists, it is my experience that neither of these requirements is likely to be met adequately, but on this point more is said in the next paragraph. Therefore the key team should consist of a technologist as leader, with a process engineer and market researcher as members. The team leader will usually require the back-up assistance of other technologists to carry out his major part of the program in formulating the product, but they should not be added to the key team because its size would then become unwieldy. A fourth key member may be added, namely, a product evaluator, when determination of performance of the new commodity is complicated beyond routine testing by the use of elaborate procedures or evaluation methods which simulate conditions of actual use.

Starting Task Force Systems

As a final point, the merits of the interdisciplinary approach are easier to see. In a cellular operation, the findings of the technologists are first turned over to a second discipline, process engineering, which nearly always reworks the process extensively to iron out the kinks, so that it can be considered suitable for large-scale operation, and for this purpose they should, but often do not, consult with the manufacturing department to get a still more practical input. After the process engineers are satisfied, they make samples by their revised method which are turned over to a third discipline, market research, the special techniques of which are used to make an estimate of market potential.

In contrast, in an interdisciplinary system the views of the process engineers and market researchers have already been injected in the product development stage, and where necessary these specialists have carried out separate tests, such as by pre-pilot work or a consumer jury, to confirm their opinions. As a result, the product concept is essentially ready for larger scale confirmation of manufacturing practicality and market development when it has survived preliminary scrutiny by process engineers and market researchers. The superiority of this interdisciplinary approach is illustrated by Chart I (page 9) which compares the feed-back relationships of a cellular organization with a task force procedure.

In spite of my preference for research and development as a test location for task forces, the experiment can be conducted in any other functional group. In earlier chapters I have indicated the makeup of interdisciplinary teams and the general nature of their activities for corporate planning and diversification, numerous other company functions, projects for public agencies, and economic development in the non-industrialized countries. In each case the proponents of the demonstration of task force methodology should follow the same course of reasoning as in the preceding paragraphs in order to develop proof of the merits of the system.

Selection of Test Projects. The demonstrations should be carried out on investigations of moderate length. If they are too short, the team members will not have had a long enough time to learn how to work together. If they are too long, the organization will be tired of waiting for some conclusions as to the workability of the system. A duration of three to four months is perhaps a good answer to both questions. If all the proposed projects appear to be very long, it is possible to separate out a particular phase as a subject.

Choice of the Team Leader. The success of a task force depends to a considerable extent on the performance of the team leader. He should be a mature, experienced individual with demonstrated ability to work with other people. He should have professional qualifications and a record of accomplishment to command the respect of his associates. While it may be preferable to select someone of not too high administrative rank for fear his views will owerawe his colleagues, his style of operation is the most important factor. He should be an excellent planner, organizer, and communicator. His work habits should be systematic. His breadth of experience and point of view are important attributes. He should have an independence of spirit, prestige, and confidence of the management to protect the operation of the task force against pressure from other executives.

Preliminary Steps for Organization of the Program. The first thing that is needed is a clear statement of the goal of the project. The outline prepared to obtain approval of the investigation may be adequate, but it should be checked to make sure that it covers the subject in sufficient detail to define the objective in terms which will provide the necessary guidance to team members. (Consultants need to check periodically the terms of their agreement with a client to make sure that they have not drifted from their commitment, and any major departure therefrom dictated by the course of the work should be negotiated anew with the client; this is a practice that is beneficial also for the management of internal task forces).

The team leader should then prepare a preliminary flow-diagram for the inputs of the different disciplines to be involved. This should not require much time, because great detail in planning is sure to be upset while the work is in progress. In fact, an experienced team leader will do this in his head.

Tentative quantification of disciplinary involvement should then be injected into this flow-diagram, and the team leader should check his estimates with the individuals he expects to invite to be team members, or at least with some source of competent opinion. Here again excessive detail should be avoided, because these are not firm commitments but only presumptive allocations of time. When the

Starting Task Force Systems

participants are accustomed to working together, the proposed schedule need not be in written form, but agreement can be reached in short informal discussions.

The final step is the organization of the task force by firm invitation to the members to serve, and clearance with their administrative superiors regarding their availability. This is all done very informally in experienced organizations, in which the give-and-take of schedules is understood. For the introduction of task force methodology, however, the proposed program of work, time involved, communications, and the like should be reached by mutual agreement.

Organization and Operation of the Task Force. With these preliminaries out of the way, the team leader usually needs to hold an organization briefing of all the participants. The goal is reviewed, the tentative schedule of the work is presented, the reporting and communication schedule is described, and any special form of interaction among disciplines is defined.

The team members then begin their actual work. The leader maintains close contact with them to follow their progress, to overcome difficulties, to revise schedules, and to maintain effective communication. He should hold frequent meetings with the key members, usually a group of three or four senior representatives of the dominant disciplines, and he should make sure that any decisions reached are properly passed on to the appropriate individuals. He may use some form of network analysis, such as a bar chart of rate of progress, to detect and correct bottle-necks. He should hold periodic coordination meetings of all members or at least most of the key participants.

The team leader and the members must rigorously defend the work against outside interference. At the same time they must maintain their freedom to seek advice or information wherever they choose.

Completion and Reporting. When work on the project appears to be complete, a wise precaution for the team leader to take is to hold a final meeting of all the members of the team. The purpose is to disclose any gaps in information, to obtain assurance that all are in substantial agreement with the findings and conclusions, and to discover any more recent developments, external as well as internal, which have a bearing on the results.

All is then ready for the leader to assemble the final report. To conserve his time, but particularly to insure accuracy, he may ask certain team members, particularly those in disciplines other than his own, to prepare drafts of their parts of the program, which he can edit into his own style of presentation. A vital section is the formulation of recommendations for future action, including the use of additional task forces to carry forward more advanced phases of the total project.

The Aftermath

This has been a demonstration project. If the initial reaction has been favorable, other task forces may have been organized. Sound managerial practice demands that the procedures be reviewed in regard to the benefits from a new form of operation.

The team leader should hold conferences — first with his key team, then with all the participants — to review the success of the methodology and to consider means by which it could be improved. The conclusions should warrant a presentation to the management to describe the advantages of this new technique. The procedures should be reviewed in general meetings of interested departments, with special sessions for those who wish to consider their adoption for their particular problems.

The organization is well on the road to the use of a new managerial tool that will speed up projects, open its structure, reduce empire building, promote the free use of its capabilities for problem solving, stimulate individual morale and initiative, and create an aggressive **climate for innovation.**

COLLATERAL READING

Most of the material in this book is based on my earlier publications, from which I have extracted the essential points. No useful purpose would, therefore, be served by reference to specific articles. This list of collateral readings includes authors cited in the text and additional relevant materials.

Books and Monographs

Allen, D.H., *A guide to the economic evaluation of projects*. The Institution of Chemical Engineers, London, 1972.

Allen, J.A., *Scientific innovation and industrial prosperity*. Elsevir, New York, 1967.

Allison, David, editor, *The R&D game: technical men, technical managers, and research productivity*. MIT Press, Cambridge, Mass., 1968.

Argyris, Chris, *Personality and organization: the conflict between system and the individual*. Harper and Row, New York, 1957.

Arnfield, R.V., and D. Roxburgh, editors, *The management of research and development*. University of Strathclyde, Glasgow, 1969; "The project team approach," J.K. O'Sullivan, pp. 9.1, 9.2; "Financial control of research and development," Lawrence W. Bass, pp. 10-1/10-17.

Baranson, Jack, *Equipment and products for developing countries*. Praeger, New York, 1969.

Bass, Lawrence W., *The management of technical programs*. Praeger, New York, 1965.

———, *Strategy for industrial development in The Lebanon*. Report of the UNDP/UNIDO senior consultant on industrial development, UNDP, Beirut, 1971.

———, *Direção de programas tecnicos*, Portuguese translation of *The management of technical programs* (1965) by André Tosello, with appendix, "A aplicação do sistema no Brasil," Fundação centro tropical de pesquisas e tecnologia de alimentos, Campinas, S.P., Brasil, 1973.

———, and Bruce S. Old, editors, *Formulation of research policies*. American Association for the Advancement of Science, Washington, 1967; "Technical programming for industrial companies," L.W. Bass and B.S. Old, pp. 197-210.

Bass, Lawrence W., see also the following author listings: George P. Bush, Carl Heyel, H.E. Hoelscher, Arthur D. Little, Inc., G.K. Manning, H.B. Maynard, National Academy of Sciences, Eugene Rabinowitch, Albert H. Rubenstein, United Nations, Universidad de Antioquia.

Bennis, Warren G., and Philip E. Slater, *The temporary society.* Harper and Row, New York, 1968.

Booz, Allen and Hamilton, *Management of new products.* Revised. Chicago, 1967.

Bryce, Murray D., *Industrial development: a guide for accelerating economic growth.* McGraw-Hill, New York, 1960.

———, *Policies and methods for industrial development.* McGraw-Hill, New York, 1965.

Bush, George P. and Lowell H. Hattery, editors, *Scientific research: its administration and organization.* American University Press, Washington, 1950; "Planning a research program," Lawrence W. Bass, pp. 47-52.

Bush, George P., and Lowell H. Hattery, *Teamwork in research.* American University Press, Washington, 1953.

Cetron, M.J., and J. Goldhar, *The science of managing organized technology.* Gordon and Breach, New York, 1970.

Commission on International Development, *Partners in development.* Praeger, New York, 1969.

Corley, H.M., editor-in-chief, *Successful commercial chemical development.* Wiley, New York, 1954.

Drucker, Peter F., *The practice of management.* Harper and Row, New York, 1954.

———, *The effective executive.* Harper and Row, New York, 1966.

Hainer, Raymond M., Sherman Kingsbury, and David E. Gleicher, *Uncertainty in research, management, and new product development.* Reinhold, New York, 1967.

Hertz, David, *The theory and practice of industrial research.* McGraw-Hill, New York, 1950.

Heyel, Carl, editor, *Handbook of industrial research management.* McGraw-Hill, New York, 1959; "Organizing for research," Sherman Kingsbury, Lawrence W. Bass, and Warren C. Lothrop, chapter 3.

Hilton, Peter, *Handbook of new product development.* Prentice-Hall, Englewood Cliffs, N.J., 1961.

Collateral Reading

Hiscocks, E.S., *Laboratory administration*. Macmillan, New York, 1956.

Hoelscher, H.E., and M.C. Hawk, editors, *Industrialization and development*, San Francisco Press, San Francisco, 1969; "Management of interdisciplinary teams from the engineering point of view" Lawrence W. Bass, pp. 371-378.

Hower, R.M., and D.C. Orth, *Managers and scientists*. Third edition. Harvard University Press, Cambridge, 1963.

Inter-American Development Bank, *Bibliographical source on industrial and technological development*. IDB, Washington, 1972.

Koontz, Harold, and Cyril O'Donnell, *Principles of management: an analysis of managerial functions*. Fourth edition. McGraw-Hill, New York, 1968; "Patterns of management analysis," chapter two. See also Fifth edition, 1972.

Likert, Rensis, *The human organization*. McGraw-Hill, New York, 1967.

Little, Arthur D., Inc., *Opportunities for industrial development in Egypt*. Report to U.S. Government Foreign Operations Administration (Earl Stafford, Lawrence W. Bass, C.S. Keevil, John C. Stephenson, et al.), Government Press, Cairo, 1955.

———, *Basic research in the Navy*. Two volumes. Report to the Naval Research Advisory Committee (Bruce S. Old, Lawrence W. Bass, et al.) U.S. National Technical Information Service, 1959.

———, *Technology behind investment*. John Walsh, Daniel P. Shedd, and Bruce M. Lane, Cambridge, Mass., 1971.

———, *Transportation and environment: synthesis for action*. (William D. Carey et al.), Cambridge, Mass., 1971.

———, *Venture simulation: a key to long-range planning*, (George B. Hegeman), Cambridge, Mass., 1971.

———, *Power to the states: mobilizing public technology*. (William D. Carey et al.), The Council of State Government, Lexington, Kentucky, 1972.

———, and Associati Pietro Gennaro Convegno, su la ricerca technica e l'organizzazione industriale, *Rivista di organizzazione aziendale*, Milano, Anno VII, N. 3, 1962; "Sviluppo storico della ricerca technica negli Stati Uniti," Lawrence W. Bass, pp. 25-32; "Definizione di 'corporate development' e delle diverse mansione techniche," pp. lv-lviii; "Fasi dello sviluppo prodotti," pp. lviii-lxi.

Lothrop, Warren C., *Management uses of research and development*. Harper and Row, New York, 1965.

McKean, Roland N., *Efficiency in government through systems analysis, with emphasis on water resource development,* Wiley, New York, 1958.

Magee, John F., *The decision tree: a guide to analyzing capital investment risks and opportunities,* ADL publication, Cambridge, Mass., 1964.

———, and M.L. Ernst, *The challenge of the future: progress in operations research.* Volume 1. Wiley, New York, 1961.

Manning, G.K., editor, *Technology transfer: successes and failures;* "Managerial aspects of technology transfer," Lawrence W. Bass, pp. 88-101; San Francisco Press, San Francisco, 1974.

Marrow, Alfred J., David G. Bowers, and Stanley J. Seashore, *Management by participation, creating a climate for organization development.* Harper and Row, New York, 1967.

Maynard, H.B., editor-in-chief, *Handbook of business administration.* McGraw-Hill, New York, 1967; "Product and process development," Lawrence W. Bass, chapter 5-3; "Plant location," Leonard C. Yaseen, chapter 7-2.

National Academy of Engineering, *Meeting the challenge of industrialization: a feasibility study for an international industrialization institute.* Washington, 1973.

National Academy of Sciences, *Research management and technical entrepreneurship.* (Panel report, K.N. Rao, Lawrence W. Bass, et al.), Washington, 1973.

———, *U.S. international firms and R, D & E in developing countries.* Washington, 1973.

National League of Cities, *National municipal policy.* Washington, 1973.

National Science Foundation, *National patterns of R & D resources: funds and manpower in the United States 1953-1973.* Washington, 1973.

Oxford University, *The role of science and technology in developing countries;* "Industrialization and research," Graham Jones, chapter 4, University Press, Oxford, U.K., 1971.

Organization for Economic Co-operation and Development, *Manual of industrial project analysis in developing countries.* 2 vol. and annex. OECD, Paris, 1968.

———, *Manual of industrial project evaluation.* OECD, Paris, 1969.

———, *Science, growth and society: a new perspecitve*, OECD, Paris, 1971.

Pelz, D.C., and F.M. Andrews, *Scientists in organizations*. Wiley, New York.

Quinn, James Brian, *Yardsticks for industrial research*. Ronald, New York, 1959.

Rabinowitch, Eugene and Victor, editors, *Views on science, technology and development*; includes "The role of technologic institutes in industrial development," Lawrence W. Bass; in press, World Development Publishing, Oxford, U.K., 1974.

Reeves, E. Duer, *Management of industrial research*. Reinhold, New York 1967.

Roberts, Edward B., *The dynamics of research and development*. Harper and Row, New York, 1965.

Rubenstein, Albert H., Theodore W. Schlie, and Alok K. Chakrabarti, *Research priorities on technology transfer to developing countries*. Northwestern University, Evanston, Ill., 1974. "The transfer of commercial systems to developing countries," Lawrence W. Bass, appendix Aa.

Ryan, J. Corboy, *Management and research management: a book of excerpts/articles*. Krieger Publishing Company, Huntington, N.Y., 1974.

Schon, Donald A., *Technology and change*. Dell, New York, 1967.

Science Council of Canada, *Innovation and the structure of Canadian industry*. Pierre L. Bourgault, Ottawa, 1972.

Servan-Schreiber, J.-J., *Le defi american*. Editions Denoel, Paris, 1967; English translation, *The American challenge*, (Ronald Steel), Atheneum, New York.

Shanks, Michael, *The innovators*. Penguin, London, 1967.

Stanley, Alexander O. and K.K. White, *Organizing the R & D function*. American Management Association, New York, 1965.

Toffler, Alvin, *Future shock*. Random House/Bantam, New York, 1970.

Tyler, Chaplin, and C.H. Winter, Jr., *Chemical engineering economics*. Fourth edition. McGraw-Hill, 1959.

Woodward, F. Neville, *Structure of industrial research associations*, OECD, Paris, 1963.

United Nations, *Manual on economic development projects.* U.N., New York, 1958. Sales No. 58. II. G.53.

———, *Manual on the management of industrial research institutes in developing countries.* (basic manuscript by Lawrence W. Bass), New York, 1966. Sales No. 66.II.B.3.

———, *Manual on the use of consultants in developing countries,* (basic manuscript by Lawrence W. Bass), U.N., New York, 1968. Sales No. E.68.II, B.10.

———, *Port administration and legislation handbook.* (U.A. Tarasca with assistance of Lawrence W. Bass), U.N., New York, 1969. Sales No. E.69.VIII.2.

———, *Industrial research institutes: guidelines for evaluation.* (Lawrence W. Bass), U.N., New York, 1971. Sales No. E.71.II.B.22.

———, *Guidelines for project evaluation.* (Partna Dasgupta, Amartya Sen, and Sephen Marglin), U.N., New York, 1972. Sales No. E.72.II.B.11.

———, *Industrial research institutes.* (I. Project selection and evaluation, Lawrence W. Bass; II. Financial administration, Robert Adams), U.N., New York, 1970. Sales No. E.70.II.B.2.

U.S. Air Force Office of Scientific Research, *Bibliography on utilization of scientific research.* Arlington, Va., 1973.

Universidad de Antioquia, *Seminaris sobra administracion de la investigacion scientifica.* Medellin, Colombia, 1969; "Sistemas para preparer projectos," Lawrence W. Bass, Doc. 1.1; El planiamiento de innovaciones, idem., Doc. 3.2.2.

U.S. Department of Commerce, *Technological innovation: its environment and management.* (J. Herbert Holleman et al.), U.S. National Technical Information Service, 1967.

Villers, Raymond, *Research and development: planning and control.* Financial Executives Research Foundation, New York, 1964.

Vollmer, Howard M., Todd R. La Porte, William C. Peterson, and Phyllis A. Langton, *Adaptations of scientists in five organizations: a comparative evaluation.* Stanford Research Institute, Menlo Park, Cal., 1964.

Journal Articles and Other References

Bass, Lawrence W., "Evaluation of technical programs," *Am. Soc. Mech. Eng.,* paper No. 50, MGT-3, 1958.

Collateral Reading 189

———, "The chemist-manager and corporate logistics," *The Chemist*, *39*, 55 (1962).

———, "Commercial development as a measure of corporate technology," Com. Chem. Deve. Assoc., preprint, 1964.

———, "The planning of innovation," *Chem. & Ind.*, London, 1967, 1671.

———, "Organization and control of research and development," *TVF*, Stockholm, 38, 245, 1967.

———, "Technologic institutes in Brazil," *Informativo do I.N.T.*, Rio de Janeiro, Año 2, No. 2, 1969.

———, "The use of composite teams to optimize problem solving," *The Bent of Tau Beta Pi*, Nashville, Tenn., 1970, April.

———, "Interdisciplinology in academe," *Chem. & Ind.*, London, 1970, 385.

———, "The role of technologic institutes in industrial development," *World Development*, vol. 1, no. 10, p. 27, 1973.

———, "The transfer of commercial systems to developing countries," *World Development*, 1974, in press.

———, and F. Neville Woodward, "The management of multidiscipline project teams," *Chem. & Ind.*, London, 1967, 1890.

Bass, Lawrence W. See also Nayudama, Y., Price, W.J.

Cairns, R.W., "Planning for research: the problems involved," *Research Management*, 4, 107, 1961.

Collier, D.W., "An innovation system for the larger company," *Research Management*, 13, 541, 1970.

Conrad, Gordon R., "Unexplored assets for diversification," *Harvard Business Review*, 41, No. 5, 1963.

———, "Diversification: the subtle strategies for success," *The Director*, 1966.

Courtney, John M., "The design concept team: linking social and physical planning," Skidmore, Owings & Merrill, Washington, 1971.

——— and Lois Dean "Joint development and multiple use of highway rights of way—a concept team approach," *Urban Law Annual*, 1970.

Cox, H.L., "The personal approach in dealing with technical people," *Research Management*, 6, 153, 1963.

Davis, Richard E., "Compatibility in corporate marriages," *Harvard Business Review, 46,* No. 4, 1968.

Drucker, Peter F., "Twelve fables of research management," *Harvard Business Review, 41,* No. 1, 1963.

Evan, W.M., "Superior-subordinate conflict in research organizations," *Administrative Science Quarterly, 10,* 52, June 1965.

Gerschinowitz, H., "Sustaining creativity against organizational pressures," *Research Management, 3,* 49, 1960.

Gibbons C.C., "The scientist as administrator," *Research Management, 6,* 425, 1963.

Gibson, R.E., "A systems approach to research management (Part 3): The operation and management of research and development organizations," *Research Management, 6,* 15, 1963.

Healey, F.H., "Job status for the research scientist" *Research Management, 3,* 239, 1960.

Hegeman, George B., "Dynamic simulation for market planning," *Chem. Eng. News,* January, 1965.

———, "Packaging management—a study in communication problems," Arthur D. Little, Inc., Cambridge, Mass., 1970.

———, "New approaches to formalized marketing planning," ADL, Cambridge, Mass., 1972.

———, "Marketing research: a look ahead, "ADL, Cambridge, Mass., 1973.

———, "The petrochemical industry in North Africa and the Middle East," ADL, Cambridge, Mass., 1973.

Heiden, C.M., "Motivating the industrial scientist," *Research Development, 14,* No. 8, 22 (1963).

Herrmann, Cyril C., and John F. Magee, "Operations research for management," *Harvard Business Review, 31,* 100, 1953.

Jenkins, D.J., "Studies in managing research and development personnel," *Research Management, 7,* 349, 1964.

Kipp, E.M., "Twelve guides to effective human relations in R & D, "*Research Management, 7,* 419, 1964.

Leamer, F.D., "Professional and administrative ladders: the advantage of broad job classification in a research organization, *Research Management, 2,* 53, 1959.

Lee, Kum-Tatt, "Utilization of local industrial research facilities by local business community and industrial enterprises," UNIDO, Vienna, 1971.

Magee, John F. "Decision trees for decision making," *Harvard Business Review, 42,* 126, 1964.

———, "Progress in the management sciences." The Institute of Management Sciences, New York, February, 1973.

———, and M.L. Ernst, "The challenge of the future: Progress in operations research," Wiley, New York, vol. 1, 1961.

Michael, S.R., "Developing managers out of creative specialists," *Research Management, 4,* 119, 1961.

Nayudama, Y., "Promoting the industrial application of research in an underdeveloped country," *Minerva, 5,* 323, 1967; comments, Lawrence W. Bass, ibid., Summer, 1967.

Pereiro de Castro, Alberto, "The utilization of local industrial research facilities by foreign concerns in developing the country," UNIDO, Vienna, 1971.

Price, William J., and Lawrence W. Bass, "Scientific research and the innovative process," *Science, 162,* 802, 1969.

Quinn, James Brian, and R.M. Cavanagh, "Fundamental research can be planned," *Harvard Business Review, 42,* 111, 1964.

———, and Robert Major, "Norway: Small country plans civil science and technology," *Science, 183,* 172, 1974.

Rubenstein, Albert H., "A program of research on the management of research development," *IEEE Transactions on Engineering Management,* September, 1966.

Sabato, Jorge A., "Quantity versus quality in scientific research (I): The special case of developing countries," *Impact of Science on Society, 20,* No. 3, 1970.

Saltzman, Arthur, "Para-transit: taking the mass out of mass transit," North Carolina A & T State University, *1972.*

Sanderson, J.P., "Draft long range plans that get results," *Business Management,* 1963.

Secrist, H.A., "Motivating the industrial research scientist," *Research Management, 3,* 57, 1960.

Shepard, H.A., "The dual hierarchy in research," *Research Management, 1,* 177, 1958.

Straus, Robert, "Departments and disciplines: stasis and change," *Science, 182,* 895, 1973.

Trussell, Paul C., "The British Colombia Research Council: A case study," UNIDO, Vienna, 1967.

Utterback, James M., "Innovation in industry and the diffusion of technology," *Science, 183,* 620, 1974.

Van Wyck, P., "The research chemist looks at the supervisor," *Reseach Management, 1,* 203, 1958.

Woodward, F. Neville, "Organization of industrial research institutes and their relationship with clients," UNIDO, Vienna, 1967.

Wright, Robert V.L., "Strategy centers: a contemporary managing system," Arthur D. Little, Inc., Cambridge, Mass., undated.

INDEX

The index is divided into three sections for the convenience of readers: I. Interdisciplinary Management; II. Uses of Task Forces; III. Name Index.

I. Interdisciplinary Management

Authority delegation, 74, 173

Benefits, 81-3
Budgetary control
   effort, 65-72
   expense, 73-4

Categories, interdisciplinary, 11-22
   comparison, 13-20
   definitions, 11-2
Cellular organizations, 8, 9, 73, 74
Colonizing research areas, 37
Committees
   comparison with task forces, 7
   management, 115-6
   of the whole, 20
Consultancy
   client-consultant relations, 121-3
   corporate development, 87
   industrial development, 156-9
   interdisciplinary practices, 4
   precautions, 121-3
   work load, 70
Corporate development: section II, 85-116
Corporate functions: section II, 7, 101-15

Emergency use, 1
Evolution, 2-7

Feasibility criteria
   corporate development, 96
   developing countries, 145-8
   products, 24-5, 39-48
   progressive use, 39-41

Industrial development: section II
Industrial operations: section II

Information retrieval, 82
Information transfer, 8, 9
Interdisciplinary teams—see also sequential teams
   authority, delegation to, 28, 177
   benefits
      individual, 82
      organizational, 81
   budgets, 21, 32, 62-72
   composition, 5, 6, 30, 45, 114-20
   concepts, 1-9
   consulting relationship, 49
   coordination, 34
   emergency use, 1
   environment, 177
   evolution, 2-7
   exploratory preparation, 26
   functional relationships, 40-74
   indoctrination, 54
   information requirement, 49
   information transfer, 8, 9, 49
   key team, 6, 29
   leader selection, 27, 118, 180
   leadership, 13, 48, 63, 65, 180
   managerial control, 61-72
   membership, 6, 119, 174-6
   objections, initial 174-7
   operation, 18, 34, 180-1
   operations research, 31-2, 119
   organization, 18, 29-31, 34, 180-1
   physical arrangements, 118
   planning, 29-31
   reporting, 36, 123, 177
   responsibility, 177
   structure, 6
   supplementary activities, 36
   use by consultants, 4

Management systems, parallel, 73-8
  activities system, 73
  organizational system, 73
Management theories, 78-81
  decision tree, 80
  empirical, 79
  human behavior, 79
  mathematical analysis, 80
  operational, 79
  social system, 80
Management development, 21, 80-3
Managerial control, 61-72
  budget, 65-72
  effort, 61-3
  major projects, 62
  minor assignments, 66
  overhead activities, 68-9
Manufacturing mobilization, 47, 59
Market forecasting, 43
Marketing mobilization, 47, 59
Mathematical models, 80
Meetings, large
  committee of the whole, 20
  control by jury, 21-2
  working groups, 21

Operations research, 32-3, 119

Pilot plants, 56
Process development, 40-52
Product development, 18-35, 39-60
Product evaluation
  consumer products, 8, 54
  industrial products, 53
Project accounting, 65-8
Project systems
  outlines, 28, 30, 31
Public projects: section II

Research, long-range
  colonizing research areas, 37
  coupling with applied projects, 35-8
  industrial, 38
Research, fundamental, 35-8
  government support
  universities
Responsibility, 74

Stages and steps in development, 50-9
  comprehensive review, 44, 58, 171
  confirmation stages, 55-8
  development stages, 51-55
  exploration, 40, 51
  implementation, 58-60
  management decision, 58
  short-cuts, 48
Starting interdisciplinary systems,
    173-82
  authority delegation, 177
  indoctrination, 180, 181
  internal environment, 177
  leader selection, 180
  managerial endorsement, 173
  objections, initial, 174-7
  operation, 181
  organization, 180, 181
  project selection, 178-80
  reporting, 181-2
  responsibility, 177
  review of operations, 182
Successive teams, 39-60
  coordination, 39
  leadership, 48-9
  membership, 40-50

Task forces, see interdisciplinary teams
Time cards
  executive, 113-5
  individual, 64-5
  initial objections, 62-3
  managerial use, 61-72

Work loads
  consultants, 70
  group, 70-2
  individual, 64-72

Index

II. Uses of Task Forces

Consultancy, 4, 87, 156-9
Corporate functions
  committee operation, 115
  development, 85-111
  development policy, 88-9
  development program, 89
  executive time distribution, 113-5
  feasibility, criteria of, 92-8
  growth plans, 88-92
  internal resources, 87-8
  meetings, internal, 118
  operations research, 31-2
  opportunities, 93-4
  planning, 85-100
  product opportunities, 86, 90-6
  product policies, 89-92
  resource appraisal, 87-8

Engineering projects, 3, 101-2

Industrial development, developing
    countries, 131-72
  case history, Lebanon, 156-9
  classification of opportunities, 114
  commercial systems transfer, 171-2
  conformance with objectives, 154-6
  development policies, 135
  development programs, 135
  entrepreneurial responsibilities,
    164-72
  environment, 131
  evaluation criteria, 145-8
  government activities, 132-4, 137-40,
    161-4, 166-70
  government focus, 131-2
  government promotion, 139-40, 161-72
  impact on economy, 152-6
  investment climate, 137
  opportunity selection, 141-54
    array of possibilities, 143
    critical evaluation, 151-2
    decision on action, 152
    evaluation criteria, 145-8
      general characteristics, 146-7
      impact on economy, 152-6
      internal suitability, 147-8

      screening, 148-50
  resource appraisal, 133-4, 147-8
  science policies, 136
  statistics, 134
  technologic institutes, 107, 138
  technology policies, 136
  technology transfer, 171-2

Industrial operations, see also
    Corporate functions
  accounting summaries, 108-9
  agricultural development, 102-3
  appraisal of opportunities, 92-100
    criteria, 92-100
    evaluation, 98
    managerial decisions, 99-100
    scoring, 96-8
    screening, 96-8
  complaints, 108
  criteria, feasibility, 96
  emergencies, 1
  engineering projects, 3, 101-2
  feasibility studies, 6, 104
  food products, 8, 26, 30, 32, 93-4, 102
  job enrichment, 110-2
  laboratory location, 102
  manufacturing scheduling, 103
  market development, 104
  market research, 110
  meetings, internal, 115
  opportunities, appraisal of, 92-100
  plant location, 102-3
  pollution abatement, 105
  process engineering, 109
  production scheduling, 103
  products, new
    classification, 90-2
    benefits and risks, 90-2
    innovative, 90-2
    items, new, 90-2
    lines, 90-2
    routine, 90-2
  quality control, 107
  repetitive tasks, enrichment, 110-2
  research and development, 4, 105-7
    aggressive, 106

      defensive, 106
      evaluation of, 105-7
   reports, 109
   sales scheduling, 103
   technical audits, 105-7
   trouble-shooting, 108
Military operations, 2-3
Public projects
   construction, 124, 126
   dams, 124
   economic development, see also developing countries, 124
   educational projects, 124
   engineering projects, 124
   fire protection, 125
   information services, 126
   legislation, 125
   police protection, 125
   pollution abatement, 125
   public health, 125
   public opinion polls, 127-9
   recreation, 125
   social benefits, 117-8
   statistics, 126
   transportation, 119, 126
   urban renewal, 126
   utilities, 125
   water utilization, 124
   welfare, 126

Surgical prostheses, 12

III. Name Index

Air Force Office of Scientific Research, 37

American Management Association, 51

Bass, Lawrence W., 21-22, 37, 156-9

Carey, William D., 117

Chamfort, Sebastian, 129

Drucker, Peter F., 19

Egyptian National Institute of Management Development (NIMD), 21, 137

Ford Foundation, 21

International Executive Service Corps, 165

Iraq, 134

Japan, 135

Koontz, Harold, 78-9

Lebanon, 132, 134, 156-9

Little, Arthur D., Inc. (ADL) xiii, 38, 105-7, 126

McKean, Roland N., 119

Magee, John F., 33, 119

Marrow, Alfred J., et al., 111

National Science Foundation, 36, 126

Naval Research Advisory Committee, 38

O'Donnell, Cyril, 78-9

Old, Bruce S., 115

Price, William J., 37

Singapore, 132

State Governments, Council of, 117, 126-7

United Nations, 144

United Nations Industrial Development Organization (UNIDO), 156-9

Yaseen, Leonard C., 102

BIOGRAPHY OF THE AUTHOR

Dr. Lawrence W. Bass has had the broad experience of seven years in fundamental research in biochemistry, fifteen years as technical director for three diversified industrial firms, and nearly thirty years as an advisor to organizations in the private and public sectors.

He was trained in chemistry at Yale: Ph. B. summa cum laude 1919, Ph. D. 1922. He carried out research on nucleic acids and proteins in France and at The Rockefeller Institute 1923-29. He was on the executive staff of Mellon Institute for eight years and has been with Arthur D. Little, Inc. since 1952. In 1942-44 he was director of a New England organization to assist small firms in converting to wartime manufactures. He was a technical director with the Borden Company, Air Reduction Company, and U. S. Industrial Chemicals; in these posts he emphasized interdisciplinary procedures.

At ADL Dr. Bass was involved chiefly in client work on the management of technology and systematic planning and strategy for organizational development. Since his retirement as a vice president in 1964 his major interest has been the problems of developing countries, with many field missions for international agencies, and in 1964 he organized and headed the first systematic training course for technical directors in Egypt. During the last two decades he has stressed the advantages and practicality of interdisciplinary techniques in his consulting relationships, writings, and lectures.

Dr. Bass is the author of four books and over 150 articles. He had major responsibility for four United Nations manuals on technical programming. In 1941 he developed with Andrew Fraser, an econometrist, for the American Chemical Society, quantitative methodology for surveys of the professional and economic status of specialized personnel; their techniques have been widely adopted. He was awarded a Presidential Certificate of Merit for his service to the military in World War II. He is past-president of the American Institute of Chemical Engineers and Yale Engineering Association and past-chairman of Engineers Joint Council.